BLUES FROM THE DELTA

WILLIAM FERRIS

Blues from the Delta

Anchor Press/Doubleday, Garden City, New York, 1978

Anchor Press edition: 1978

Parts of this book have appeared, in slightly different form, in William Ferris' BLUES FROM THE DELTA, published in England in 1970.

All photographs in this book are from the collection of the author. Permission to reproduce must be obtained through the publisher.

Grateful acknowledgment is made for permission to reprint excerpts from the following material:

> "Ain't That Lovin' You Baby" by Jimmy Reed. Copyright © 1955 by Conrad Music.

> "Big Boss Man" by Al Smith and Luther Dixon. Copyright © 1960 by Conrad Music and Unart Music Corp.

> "Crying in the Chapel" by Artie Glenn. Copyright © 1953 by Valley Publishers, Inc. All rights controlled by Unichappell Music, Inc. (Belinda Music, publisher). International Copyright Secured. ALL RIGHTS RESERVED. Used by permission.

> "Rock Me Momma" by Arthur "Big Boy" Crudup. Copyright © 1944 by Wabash Music Company.

> "Sunny Road" by Roosevelt Sykes. Copyright 1946 by Wabash Music Company.

Library of Congress Cataloging in Publication Data

Ferris, William R
  Blues from the Delta.

  Bibliography: p. 195
  Discography: p. 205
  Filmography: p. 221
  1. Blues (Songs, etc.)—Mississippi—History and criticism. 2. Afro-American musicians—Mississippi. I. Title.
ML3561.B63F47 1978   784
ISBN: 0-385-09918-5
Library of Congress Catalog Card Number 75–36622

For Poppa Jazz
1903–1974

CONTENTS

ACKNOWLEDGMENTS   ix

PREFACE   xi

I BLUES ROOTS   1

Entering the Delta   3

The Blues Family   11

The Blues Perspective   25

Early Sounds   31

Learning the Blues   37

Talking the Blues   41

Blues Generations   45

Records   51

II BLUES COMPOSITION   55

Make Ups   61

Verses   67

Blues Proverbs   73

Blues Conjuration   77

Bluesmen and Preachers   79

Black and White Music 91

The White Audience 95

III BLUES HOUSE PARTY 99

Blues Talk 107

The House Party 115

IV LETTERS 157

NOTES 179
BIBLIOGRAPHY 195
DISCOGRAPHY 205
FILMOGRAPHY 221

ACKNOWLEDGMENTS

Blues from the Delta began as my folklore dissertation which Kenneth Goldstein directed at the University of Pennsylvania. Parts of the dissertation were published in 1970 under the same title, and since then field work with musicians and correspondence with blues scholars have expanded and reshaped my earlier study.

My understanding of black culture and the blues has grown through long conversations and correspondence with John Blassingame, B. B. King, Alan Lomax, Paul Oliver, and Robert Farris Thompson. To each I owe a special debt.

Close readings and valuable suggestions on this text were offered by David Evans, Barry Pearson, Larry Powell, Diane Rose, Susan Steinberg, and Jeff Titon. David Evans and Frank Scott provided extensive references on the recorded sources of performances and the discography. Careful tune transcriptions, identification of tale types, and typing were done by Marty Kluger, Joan Perkal, and Ann Granger respectively, while Marie Brown, John Ware, and Wendy Weil shepherded the text through editorial channels. My field research was supported by the National Endowment for the Arts, National Endowment for the Humanities, National Science Foundation, Rockefeller Foundation, and Wenner-Gren Foundation.

The book is shaped by men and women in the Mississippi Delta who unveil the blues world through their conversations and performances, and my greatest debt is clearly to Shelby "Poppa Jazz" Brown, Wallace "Pine Top" Johnson, Lee Kizart, Jasper Love, Maudie Shirley, and James "Son" Thomas.

William Ferris
Yale University
October 1977

PREFACE

Blues shape both popular and folk music in American culture, and blues-yodeling Jimmie Rodgers, Elvis Presley, and the Rolling Stones are among many white performers who incorporate blues in their singing styles. Though a contemporary blues artist like B. B. King is familiar to audiences throughout the world, few listeners are aware of either King's life or the history of his music. Lacking a sense of the historical and artistic dimension of blues, their public often romanticizes the music.

This study views the blues as it developed in the Mississippi Delta. From the first records issued in the 1920s to contemporary sounds by B. B. King, Muddy Waters, and Howlin' Wolf, the Delta has produced an uninterrupted musical tradition which is still sung by little-known Delta performers. My work is dedicated to these singers.

From 1967 to 1976 I recorded performances and interviews with Delta bluesmen. In the pages that follow, they explain how records and a new generation of singers and musicians are reshaping earlier blues styles. The singers show how they compose lyrics for performances at local house parties and "jook joints." And they all immerse us in their music as they reminisce, explain, and play the blues.

The extraordinary range and importance of their music is also shown in the extensive books, recordings, and films on blues included at the end of the study.

BLUES (blōōz), n. (short for *blue devils.*) 1. *Colloq.* Low spirits; a fit of melancholy. 2. A type of song written in a characteristic key with melancholy words and syncopated rhythms.

Webster's New Collegiate Dictionary

Blues consists of a (three-line) twelve-bar pattern. Each line of the verse corresponds to four measures of the music. To express it in another way, there are two complete melodic statements (corresponding to the verse statement and its repetition), each ending on the tonic (or the third or fifth of the tonic chord), followed by the melodic "response" (corresponding to the third line of the verse), which also ends on the tonic.

Gilbert Chase, *America's Music*

Blues actually is around you every day. That's just a feeling within a person, you know. You have a hard time and things happen. Hardships between you and your wife, or maybe you and your girlfriend. Downheartedness, that's all it is, hardship. You express it through your song.

Arthur Lee Williams
Blues Harmonica Player
Birdie, Mississippi

BLUES FROM THE DELTA

I   BLUES ROOTS

Entering the Delta

I walked sixty-one highway till I give down in my knees
Trying to find somebody to give my poor heart ease.

James Thomas, Leland, Mississippi

Highway 61 stretches across two hundred miles of rich black
land known as the Mississippi Delta where mile-long rows of
cotton and soybeans spread out from its pavement and surround
occasional towns such as Lula, Alligator, Panther Burn, Nitta
Yuma, Anguilla, Arcola, and Onward. The flat Delta land ex-
tends from Memphis, Tennessee, to Vicksburg, Mississippi, and
is defined by loess bluffs on its eastern edge and the Mississippi
River on its west. For centuries the river has overflowed its
banks each spring, and desposits of alluvial soil are thirty feet
deep in some areas.

Until 1820 the Delta was an undeveloped "island" whose fer-
tile soil was covered with dense hardwood forests, great cane
brakes, and bayous. Settlers began to develop the Delta as part
of the expanding cotton empire around 1835, and after the Civil
War its land was cleared and plantations developed with black
labor. One writer described the region as "cotton obsessed,
Negro obsessed, and flood ridden, it is the deepest South, the
heart of Dixie, America's super-plantation belt."[1]

During the post-Civil War period, thousands of black freedmen migrated to the Delta to clear and farm its fields. They were
recruited by labor agents who promised higher wages and civil
rights which had been lost in other parts of the state. The Delta
economy was founded upon the labor of blacks who cleared
fields, built levees to protect them from floods, and cultivated

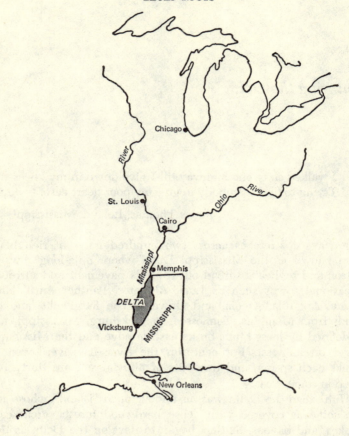

their crops.² As late as the 1930s, Jasper Love, a Clarksdale blues singer, worked with mules to clear and farm the land, and daily labor began and ended with the toll of the farm bell.

> Times was so tough we couldn't cut it with a knife, man. Plowing four mules and one of these "true blue" middle busters or "yellow jackets." Hitting them stumps and that plow kicking you all in the stomach. I had to git up around three in the morning by a bell. The bell rang two times. First time you git up. The second time, be at the barn. Not on your way, at the barn.³

Black sharecroppers complained that they always ended the farm year in debt. Their crop could never pay the cost of land rental, mules, and supplies, and final settlement with the white landowner was a familiar scene.

All right, you start picking cotton and about settling time you done picked out about twenty-five bales of cotton and go in to settle. He'd pop his finger on you when you walk in.

"Joe, I sat up all night trying to figure things out.

Here you done made twenty-five bales of cotton. I just don't want to tell you, Joe, hard as you worked. I don't want to tell you. Here. Smoke a cigarette."

He's setting at the table and ain't got nothing on the table but money. You think you gonner git it? Out of the question. He'd set there and he'd figure and he'd figure, and when he git through, he'd pop his finger again.

"Looka here. If you'd have made one more bale of cotton, this is what you'd of had as your part. Joe, I just ain't got the heart to tell you. How much you want to borrow?"

He'd loan you about twelve or thirteen hundred dollars. Now this thirteen hundred dollars what he loaning you, you done made that already, but he done popped his finger on it.[4]

Because of such conditions many black families left the Delta in this century, following highways 51 and 61, which linked their towns with northern industrial centers like St. Louis and Chicago. Singers also followed these routes, and their verses reflect the map of highways leading north. Standing on Delta soil, the bluesman sings about "going to" Chicago or "leaving" Tutwiler, towns with urban and rural associations for the blues audience.

After 1940 blacks increasingly moved north in large numbers seeking better jobs and living conditions. Between 1955 and 1960 60 per cent of the black migrants to Chicago were from the South, and three fourths of these were Mississippi-born.[5] For Shelby Brown and many other Delta residents, Chicago became a symbol of escape from the rural South.

One thing about Chicago, people told me that money was even growing on trees there. I went and got me two sacks to carry with me for that money tree in Chicago. I went there and my brother, he saw me with two sacks. He say, "Shelby, what you carrying them sacks for?"

I said, "Man, I'm looking for that money tree that's here in Chicago."

They told me about the money tree and I was looking at every tree and didn't see no money. So he say, "Look, man, there ain't no money growing on trees."

So he grabbed the sacks and throwed them in the garbage can and said, "Don't do that. You let the folks make a fool out of you. Chicago is a free place, but don't come and look for money on the tree. They'll know you ain't nothing but a country fool."

I stayed there thirteen years and then I come back home to Leland. It got too rough in Chicago.[6]

Like Shelby Brown, many families moved back and forth between Chicago and Mississippi, and today blacks still outnumber whites in the Delta by two to one. Most of the population lives in small towns of fewer than five hundred inhabitants with a main street which contains the local bank, post office, assorted stores, and restaurants. The Main Street is a point of reference when discussing sections of the town, and people living across it are referred to as "staying over in" that particular section. Black neighborhoods have names like "Black Dog" and "Brick Yard" which only natives understand. These neighborhoods are clearly separated from white areas, and when one passes from black to white areas the difference is visible in more expensive homes and their landscape. The lawns and flower gardens of wealthy whites are often maintained by blacks whose homes are very different.

Most blacks live in rental property and it is not unusual to find eight or ten people living in a three-room house. Rows of shotgun houses are common in black neighborhoods where homes are crowded together with occasional small trees—often chinaberry—planted for shade. Hard, bare earth around the house provides a playground for children, and women "sweep out" their yard with a broom as an extension of the home.

Blacks in these homes depend on manual skills for their income, and with the mechanization of farm work steady jobs are difficult to find. Men work part time on farms and seek out other jobs around town. Chinese, Syrian, and Italian merchants in the neighborhoods often live above their grocery stores.[7] Since few gardens exist in towns, supplies are bought in these stores, and the lore of Delta blacks deals with merchants who are not considered "white men" or "American." Jasper Love identified Anglo-Saxons as "white men" and excluded minority groups such as Italians.

> I remember I was in Chicago. . . . I got a job out in Cicero. . . . Most of them was Italians, not white men. You hardly catch a white man working in Chicago. They most was Italians. They was good guys.[8]

For at least eighty years, Delta towns like Tutwiler, Moorhead, and Louise have produced a steady flow of blues singers whose music is now internationally known. W. C. Handy made handsome profits playing for dances and political rallies around Clarksdale at the turn of the century and attributed his support to the rich Delta soil.

> I made more money in Clarksdale than I had ever earned. This was not strange. Everybody prospered in that Green Eden. Cotton stalks here were as tall as Alabama corn. Delta land yielded three or four bales to one produced on the same amount of hill land. The cotton rows that I had seen around Florence [Alabama] were downright scrawny by comparison.[9]

From the first issues of "race" records in the 1920s, Delta blues singers were widely recorded, and some of the best-known names were Son House, Bukka White, Arthur "Big Boy" Crudup, Robert Johnson, and Charley Patton. More recent blues stars such as Muddy Waters, Howlin' Wolf, and B. B. King are also from the Delta.[10]

If we "map" the blues in Mississippi, the Delta clearly has the greatest concentration of towns in which singers were either born or lived for extended periods.[11] Other important blues areas are south of Jackson along Highway 51 and in Jackson where singers such as Son House, Skip James, and Charley Patton were located for recording companies by Henry Speir.[12]

Jasper Love remembers when the first record players appeared in the Delta. Some black listeners felt they were the white man's way of spying on blacks in their homes and refused to talk when a record was playing.

I remember I had a old record player with a bulldog on it. One of them antiques, you know, that you wind. That dog would sit up there while that record was playing Bessie Smith, Blind Lemon, and all that.

They told them, "Don't be talking while you listening at that record player because the white man'll hear if you say something."

They might just say, "That's a good record," because that [white] man had them fooled that he could hear them through that dog and hear what they say. In other words the peoples just really believed that.[13]

From the traditional blues of the '20s to contemporary rhythm-and-blues styles, singers from the Delta have played a major role in shaping the blues sound. Music was one of the few avenues to success available for blacks, and because blues records were sold to black audiences, recording success reflected how well a singer expressed the feelings of his or her audience. The blues singer became a spokesman for the black community, and the number of nationally known artists from the Delta indicates the importance of their music to black culture as a whole. Their music expresses the feelings of a people segregated by Jim Crow laws, and through the blues they speak of a dream to "set the whole nation right."

In Washington they called me and I went.
I had to be a guest of the president.
He said "Come on in here, mighty glad you come in here.
"I want you to help me run the Russians out the Western hemisphere."
I said "You can run the country, I'm gonner run the city,
"Gonner be some changes, though, for the true soul brothers here,
"Ray Charles and Lightning Hopkins, and a guy like Jimmy Reed,
"Bo Diddley and Big Maybelle all I need."
I had a dream, dream I had last night.
I dreamed I went to the U.N. and set the whole nation right.[14]

The Blues Family

When I began my study of blues in 1967 I was told by a white that it was "past strange" for a white Mississippian like myself to record blacks in their homes. It was impossible to maintain rapport with both whites and blacks in the same community, for the confidence and cooperation of each was based on their feeling that I was "with them" in my convictions about racial taboos of Delta society. When whites presented me to blues singers, our discussions were limited to non-controversial topics, as performers felt my tapes would be replayed before other whites in the community. In fact, local whites who provided contacts were suspicious of my work and often asked to hear the tapes. I carefully avoided playing anything controversial and their assistance so restricted my relationship with performers that I later began to enter black communities on my own.[15]

One introduction marked the last time I approached blacks through local whites. A white farmer agreed to let me record a blues player who worked for him and told me I should come to the performer's home that evening. I arrived and found the farmer and several other whites were also there. All had guns which hung from rear-window racks in their pickup trucks and were standing together admiring a rifle when I arrived. When the farmer saw me, he called the player by throwing rocks on his tin roof. The singer came out and sang several songs on his front porch while the whites watched him from their trucks. He then complained his finger was too cramped to play any more, and when the whites left I made an appointment to meet him again.

The following night the musician played at length and toward the end of the recording session he became intoxicated, cursed his white boss, and told me that he really owned the farm where he worked. He said the next time I came to town I should eat and sleep at his home and swore I would be safe with his family.

> Next time you come, come on to my house and walk right in. If I eat a piece of bread, you eat too. I'm the boss of that whole place over there. I don't know how many acres it is. You ain't got to ask none of these white folks about coming to my house. Anytime you come to my house and I ain't there, stay right there till I come. Don't leave. I'm coming back, cause I'm going to git some pussy and I'll be back in a minute. Any time you want to come down here, you drive to my damn house. Ain't a damn soul gonner fuck with you, white or black.[16]

After this incident, I approached blacks directly and found that as long as I remained in their section of town I could work freely and effectively without interference from local whites.[17] When local police stopped and questioned me I showed my Mississippi identification and was never arrested.

There were always exceptions to the patterns of segregation which stood out. While I interviewed Arthur Lee Williams, a harmonica player near Birdie, his white neighbor's children arrived for dinner. Williams explained that his children took their supper with the white family, and on weekends they sometimes picnicked and fished together.

Black families constantly extended their hospitality by offering to feed and house me as long as I was in their neighborhood. When I entered a black home and shared a meal with the family, I broke racial taboos engrained from childhood in the lives of white and black Southerners. In response, the black community accepted the integrity of my work and did everything possible to assist me. I became a friend rather than a "white man," and teenagers on the street called me "soul brother" or "brother." With this rapport, I recorded protest material which would have been concealed had I not been accepted as a friend sympathetic with the racial perspective expressed in their lore.

Often during the telling of a racial joke directed against whites, I felt eyes were following my response at points of humor. My laughter indicated a sympathy with the black protagonist in the joke and helped establish our friendship. Once I moved into the black community and exposed myself to the threat of white society, I could enter blues "jook joints" and record freely.[18]

Before recording I explained my work clearly and asked musicians if they would like to be a part of a project which would preserve their blues traditions. They were surprised that a book could be written about people and songs that were a part of daily life which they assumed had little interest outside their own community.

I often bought groceries for families in exchange for their hospitality. Another favor which seemed to touch people more than gifts of food were photographs of musicians which I mailed with a letter of thanks for their help. When I returned to communities for further work, I was repeatedly touched by the effect of my letters.

I usually recorded in black neighborhoods of small towns where my presence was less noticeable, and experiences in Leland suggest the pattern of my field work. I found a black cafe and asked an older man if there were any blues singers in the area. He replied, "Well, you might talk to Son Thomas. His real name is James Thomas but he go by 'Son' or 'Cairo.'"

Nicknames are given by the community, and those of blues singers usually relate to their music. Nicknames such as "Pine Top," "Cairo," and "Poppa Jazz" are more important than surnames and often when I inquired after actual names no one recognized the person. I searched for William and Iola Jones for half a day before someone recognized them as "Jug Head" and "Don't Know No Better." The latter name was given because of Iola's strange walk, and their friend "Night Duck" was so named "'cause he do more traveling at night than in the day. He go anywhere and don't be scared of nothing."[19]

I found "Son" Thomas's home in a neighborhood known as "Black Dog" and asked his wife, Christine, if he was in. She said no one named James Thomas lived there, and asked why I wanted him. When I explained I was writing a book on the blues and wanted to include him in it, she admitted she was his wife and told me how I could find him.

I soon found Thomas and began a friendship which deepened throughout the summer. A good measure of our rapport was the response of his children, who were always more direct than their parents in showing their feelings toward me. When I first entered their home, they avoided me and rarely spoke in my presence. Later, after I had spent many hours with their father, the children would run to the door and, holding my hands, lead me into their home, telling jokes and stories they wanted to record. They often held my hands while I spoke with Son about his music.

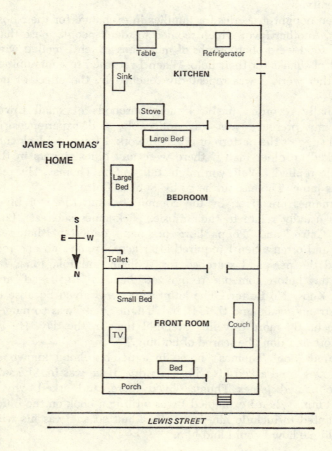

James Thomas, his wife, and ten children lived in a three-room "shotgun" house.[20] In the front room two beds and a couch faced a television which played throughout the day. The center room served as a bedroom, and the kitchen was at the rear. Children constantly moved in and out of the home while Mrs. Thomas explained how they each slept.

> We have ten kids, six girls and four boys. And we have two large beds and a small bed and the couch. The oldest girl, she sleeps on the couch. Me and Son and the two baby girls, we sleeps in the large bed, and the next biggest girl, the two little ones, and the four boys sleeps there in that bed. Uh huh.[21]

It was some time after our first meeting that Son sang blues with strong racial themes such as "Smoky Mountain Blues."

God forgive a black man most anything he do.
God forgive a black man most anything he do.
Now I'm dark-complexioned, looks like he'd forgive me too.[22]

Just as the children showed their trust through physical touch, Son and his friends showed theirs by letting me record stories and songs which increasingly used protest and obscenity (see chapter on Verses).[23]

Expression of affection through physical touch was characteristic of the black community. Son took me to Kent's Alley and the home of his friend, Shelby "Poppa Jazz" Brown, who ran a blues joint for over thirty years. We shook hands and afterward Gussie Tobe, a friend of Poppa Jazz's, asked me, "Do you know what you just shook?"

"No. What?"

"A handful of love."

This warmth and verbal banter was repeated whenever Tobe came to Poppa Jazz's home. Poppa Jazz was sixty-four, and when he spoke, he walked around the room dramatically gesturing and making boasts and threats before his seated audience. Once Tobe turned to me and said, "I want you to whip Jazz's ass for

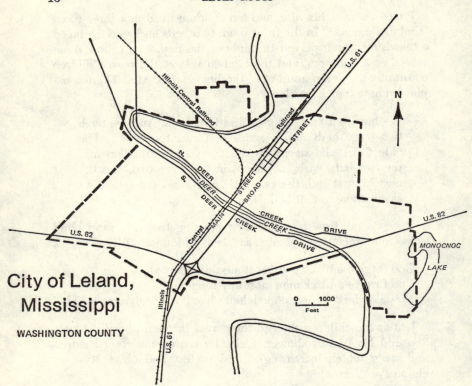

City of Leland,
Mississippi

WASHINGTON COUNTY

me. If you don't I'm gonner go home for my shotgun and shoot
the son of a bitch dead."

Poppa Jazz turned to me and said, "I'm waiting for him. I'm
waiting for him."

He stood shirtless and walked around with his chest pushed
forward. Tobe whispered loudly to me, "You wouldn't think that
man's eighty and can walk around sometime without his cane."

Poppa Jazz answered, "Watch your mouth 'cause I'm your
daddy, boy. I'm your daddy."

Son then mentioned he had to dig a grave the next day for the
white funeral home where he worked, and Shelby replied, "Another rich one gone. Boy, you gonner have plenty of money.
Lend me a dollar."

Poppa Jazz was living with a woman he had married thirty

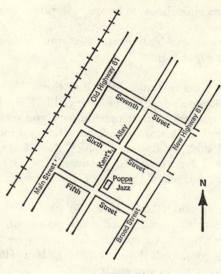

CITY OF LELAND

years earlier who had just returned after a twenty-year separation. While I was in their home a local woman who had "stayed
with" Poppa Jazz for seven years dropped by and seemed surprised to see his wife there. The visitor asked Mrs. Brown a number of questions about her relation with Poppa Jazz, and when
she left, Mrs. Brown turned to me and said, "I told her quick
who was running this house. She must have thought I was just a
whore he picked up."

Mrs. Brown later told me of her experiences with the Civil
Rights Movement and how she organized voter registration in
her home town. Because of her bravery she was selected to par-
ticipate in the March on Washington in 1963 and described her
experiences in detail.

Poppa Jazz saw that I listened to his wife sympathetically and
began to tell me of the injustices he had known as a young man
in Leland. He said blacks were considered "crazy" when they
retaliated against a white. He left the South as a young man and

lived in northern cities because he was too proud to accept white intimidation.

He recalled one incident during his youth when he bought peanuts from a white man.

> I wasn't nothing but a little boy then. That was in 1912 and I wasn't but eleven years old. They had this place that cooked peanuts outside, and you could smell them all over the town. I didn't have but one nickel that day and I told my friend, I said, "Man, I want some peanuts, and I'm scared to go over here to get them 'cause this man, when he sell you the peanuts, he kicks you."
>
> My friend said, "Man, look. Go and give him the nickel. Get them peanuts and when you hand him the nickel, don't take your eye off him. When he raise his foot to kick you, grab it and that'll trip him. His head'll hit that concrete and you got it made."
>
> So sure nuff I went on and give the man a nickel for the peanuts. When he aimed to kick me with his foot, I grabbed it, and his head hit the concrete. His momma was setting near him in a big chair, and she says, "The nigger killed my boy. Done killed my boy."
>
> Then all the white folks grabbed me. They put a gun on me and whipped me cause I did that. That night I walked that railroad all night with a Winchester, but I didn't see nothing. If I had of seen anything white like a chicken it would of been too bad. After that they called me the "Shotgun Kid."[24]

Poppa Jazz recalled an old black man who killed the sheriff in Leland. After witnessing his fate, Jazz moved north to Chicago. Later, he described the incident to me;

> He was an old man and didn't live in no house. He stayed out in the woods, and he would come and get his hair cut in town. So one time he come to get his hair cut, and he went in there with a shotgun. Always carried a shotgun everywhere he'd go. He stood the

shotgun in the corner to git him a hair trim and a shave, and when he got out of the chair to look for his shotgun, it was gone. He said, "Somebody done got my gun."

So they give it to him and he hit the railroad going back to where he stayed at in the woods. When the sheriff heard about him and the shotgun he went out there to get him, and the old man killed him. I was grazing my cows in that pasture and saw it with my eyes. Didn't nobody tell me nothing. I saw it.

When they finally got the old man, they put him in a box and carried him up there in front of the pool room. They put four crossties on top of the box and poured five gallons of gasoline over it. When they started the fire, it blowed up and the old man come out of there running. He run right here to the hotel, and they got him again and put a rope around his neck and hung him where the red light is right now. The first red light in town. When they hung him there, I was on the railroad looking. They said, "Boys, get off the railroad."

I didn't go nowhere. I stood there looking. All my brothers and sisters was looking at him too, those what was big enough to see it. I left here after I saw all that stuff, 'cause I didn't want them to kill me. I figured next time it was gonner be me. They didn't like me 'cause I'd fight. I'd kill anybody, white or black.[25]

Poppa Jazz concluded, "In those days it was 'Kill a mule, buy another. Kill a nigger, hire another.' They had to have a license to kill everything but a nigger. We was always in season."

Poppa Jazz's home was a familiar part of the Leland blues community. His four-room house stood on Kent's Alley between Fifth and Sixth streets. Set between "old" and "new" Highway 61, it was the heart of what James Thomas calls "the rough part of town."

During the day visitors moved in and out of the home buying corn whiskey and asking which musicians would play that evening. Those who stayed to talk and tell stories sat with Poppa Jazz in the front bedroom which faced Kent's Alley and gave

POPPA JAZZ'S HOME

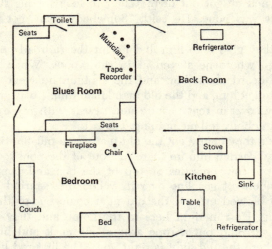

POPPA JAZZ'S BLUES ROOM

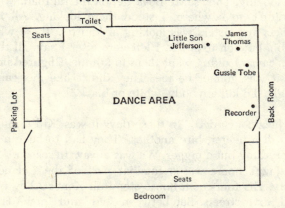

Jazz a full view of activities outside. Often Jazz would tell a story, then rush to a window to check the alley, declaring, "No bullshit. I ain't lying either. I ain't lying."

When night came, activity shifted to the back of the home as singers and dancers gathered in his blues room. The room was dimly lit, and there were no lights in the adjacent room, where corn whiskey was chilled in a refrigerator. Poppa Jazz usually stood in the door between the two rooms and personally led customers to the refrigerator when they needed a drink.

His main guitarist, James Thomas, played in a back corner beneath a calendar with a color picture of Jesus and his disciples. "Little Son" Jefferson sat on Thomas's right and accompanied him on the harmonica. When asked how long they would play, Thomas replied, "Till late hours of midnight."

Guests sat around the room on chairs and a large couch or danced in its center. James Thomas was the main attraction, and as the evening progressed, the audience became more responsive to his music. Women would answer his blues line, "You don't love me, Baby" with "Yes I do, Daddy."

Poppa Jazz moved constantly serving whiskey, talking to visitors in the blues room, and leaning out its side door to encourage groups in the parking lot to come in. Occasionally he danced alone or performed a toast in front of Thomas, then resumed selling whiskey. Jazz knew his customers well, and those prone to fighting were closely watched and asked to leave if they became too loud. After escorting a man out the door he turned to me and said, "That was a bad one. They tell me a woman shot his nuts off in Chicago."

Bluesmen like Arthur "Poppa Neil" O'Neil, Joe Cooper, and Eddie Quesie might play while Thomas rested, but they never replaced him as the main performer. When a third singer arrived he would sit on Thomas's left and wait for a break in the music. Gussie Tobe sometimes sat in the third chair and sang his composition, "The Ohio River Bridge."

It was early one morning, when the bridge come tumbling down.
I say it was early one morning, when that bridge come tumbling down.
Well that Ohio River Bridge was tumbling down.
I told Cairo [Thomas], oooh, when the bridge was tumbling down.
I was out there that morning when that bridge come tumbling down.

On that Monday morning, Baby, even that Wednesday morning too.
We was working out there, I told the man in his office,
I said "Look here, Mr. Mare," I said. "The bridge is tumbling down."

Say, you know where I was at? Leland, Mississippi. Down here at Jazz's place. Yeah![26]

In the midst of this scene the blues community grew like a family with a kinship of love for music and good times shared together.[27] Until his death in 1974, Poppa Jazz was the central figure who held the Leland family together. As his name suggests, he became a father to aspiring singers like James Thomas, who was raised by grandparents in Eden. Thomas remembers how he first came to Leland on Saturday nights to visit his mother and sister.

> On Saturday nights, that would usually be the night that I'd come to Leland. I'd get off the bus and go and see my mother and sister there. Then I would go round to Shelby's club and he'd have boys around there playing the guitar. I'd go around and play some with them and then come back to the house.
>
> Shelby was a big man then. He had plenty of money. He'd hold his head way high then and talk loud. He'd have men hanging around there playing the guitar and everybody'd meet up there on Sunday for big jokes and drinking. They'd have a nice time round there.

Poppa Jazz:
> That's true. Yeah, that's true. He ain't joking none. When I'd see Son coming I'd be glad. It was just like that all night long. You know, we didn't go to bed. Them there gals hung around me, you know, with that good liquor and stuff. They liked that. I started a jazz band and they started to calling me "Poppa Jazz." Well, James, he come here. I knowed his mother and sister

and all of them here, you know. And he came here one
night. I had a joint open down there called the "Rum
Boogie." He said, "I'm gonner play a number."

"What's your name?"

"James."

I said, "Go on. I know you."

I knowed who he was. So he went on that stage and
everybody liked him. I said, "Buddy, when you come
back through here, you stop."

So every time Son would come, he'd come over here
and look for my guitar. He could play it. I'd be looking
for him, too. That was when I named him "Cairo." You
see at Cairo the water got so high, and he played that
blues:

> I would go to Cairo, but the water too high for me.
> The girl I love, she got washed away.

He really rapped it. Everybody liked it. Every time
folks see me, "Hey, man, you seen Cairo?"

"No, but he'll be here tonight."

"We'll be back then."

They sure did come. They liked to hear him play, and
he could play all them kind of blues. I loved the blues
all my life. That's all I ever liked. And I ain't but forty-
one.

James Thomas:

I'm mighty 'fraid that's his house number [Laughter].
Little Son Jefferson and me, we would sing our theme
song to welcome everybody to Jazz's place. We called
him "Mr. Shelby."

> Good evening, Everybody.
> Peoples, tell me how do you do.
> Well we just come out this evening,
> Just make a welcome with you.
> Well it's all on the counter.

People, it's all on the shelf.
Well if you don't find it at Mr. Shelby's place,
People, you can't find it nowhere else.

Then when we got ready to close down the place we would sing:

Good bye, Everybody.
You know we got to go.
Good bye, Everybody.
People, you know we got to go.
But if you come back to Mr. Shelby's place,
You will see the same old show.[28]

The Blues Perspective

I remember my daddy, he would call hisself singing on
the blues side. He'd be plowing the mule and git hot,
and you'd hear him out there in the field hollering "I'm
going up to the bayou, baby, and I can't carry you."

Jasper Love, Clarksdale, Miss.

A lone man singing the blues is an appropriate beginning. For
from Africa to slavery, from southern farms to northern ghettos
the musician is ever present. African griots, slave singers, and
country and urban bluesmen share a common musical tradition
as their lyrics speak of movement across land and water and the
singer's separation from loved ones.[29] The bluesman's poetry
evokes memories of slavery, Reconstruction, and the Jim Crow
South. In each period musicians spoke for their people by singing about their lives.

I'm drifting and I'm drifting just like a ship out on the sea.
You know I ain't got nobody in this world to care for me.[30]

Asked to define the blues, Jasper Love recalls scenes of hard
labor and personal loneliness.

I've heard my grandmother say it was a boat they
called the *Choctaw*. She say she used to roll a whole
barrel of syrup or molasses. She used to roll them bar-
rels right alongside of her husband, and she used to cut

sprouts with him when they was cleaning up. Those
blues come from way back when they had to study
something to try to give them some consolation. The
man was doing them so bad, taking all they had and
working them to death. They just had to do something,
so they sang about what they felt.[31]

To express these feelings through song is to sing the blues. As
thoughts roll across his mind, the blues singer defines a perspective which makes sense of black life by focusing his verses on
themes which recur in both conversation and performance.[32]

Numerous verses on race remind us that a common history
binds the performer and his audience. The singer consciously assumes his role as a black man singing for his own color, and
blues intensify this racial identity. B. B. King stresses, "If you've
been singing the blues as long as I have, it's kind of like being
black twice."[33] Blues draw their audience into the reality of
blackness as James Thomas uses humor to develop verses about
racial tension.

> Nigger and white man playing seven up.
> Nigger beat the white man, scared to pick it up.
> He had to bottle up and go.[34]

As female vocalists recall low-down men, and male singers
complain of their women, each sex feels the other is responsible
for their blues and focuses its verses accordingly. When men and
women vocalists sing together, a call and response session often
develops in which a sexual perspective is clear. In the following
verses Pine Top Johnson and Maudie Shirley sing about how
each has been mistreated by the other.

Pine Top begins:
> Listen here, Woman, where'd you stay last night?
> You know you ain't treating me right.
> Aw, Woman, you steady running wild.
> Now the baby I'm loving, she don't treat me right.

And Maudie replies:
When I stay at home every day, trying to treat you right,
You come home late at night, jump on me and there's a fight.
Baby, you know that ain't right.

Pine Top:
What's that, Baby?

Maudie:
You heard me![35]

This male-female session shows the strong male-female perspective in blues, and similar sexual exchanges have been recorded by popular blues and rhythm and blues singers.[36] This call and response pattern also appears in solo performances where singers address their guitar as a woman, and the guitar's strings give a musical reply. B. B. King and his guitar, "Lucille," is the best-known example of this tradition.

During the early period of blues recordings, female vocalists like Ma Rainey and Bessie Smith were active in urban areas, while singers recorded from the rural South were largely male.[37] The perspective of rural blues is usually male, and when I asked James Thomas where blues come from, he replied, "Where they come from? They come from mens, all I know."

For the male singer lost love becomes a rite of passage as he remembers his woman and consoles himself through music. James Thomas explains the pain he felt when his wife left him while he was working in a log field:

I come in that evening and I'd bought a pack of cigarettes. A little boy told me, said, "Your wife gone," and I got sick all at once.

I said, "I know she's gone."

"She carried all her clothes with her."

"I know it, boy. Git on away from here."

Well that hurts, you know. When she left, that messed me up for a long time, and it don't take much

for that feeling to hit me. When it does I just can't rest.
I have to walk or ride or do something.

I used to sing a song about "When my first wife quit
me, she put me on the road." Well, you think of her
while you're singing. Plenty of times I would be thinking about her, you know, while I'd be playing.

That's what you call a "deep study." That means
thinking about how some woman done treated you. You
want her and she don't want you. That's what the blues
is made up about.[38]

Religion also shapes the blues for singers often define their
music in relation to the church. Though some churchgoers associate blues with the devil, blues singers call on the Lord for support in their verses, and audiences encourage the performer
to "preach the blues." Blues singers feel their music describes life
as it is, with an honesty not found in the church. Consecrated
with wine and dance, their performance is a secular service
which embraces not only the Sabbath but the complete week.

Rural singers have a strong sense of place in their music, and
their verses celebrate towns like Moorhead "where the Southern
crosses the Dog" and "Vicksburg on the high hill, Natchez just a
little below." The terms "country" and "urban" blues suggest
how clearly a sense of place defines their musical form. B. B.
King's "Why I Sing the Blues" describes Chicago's ghetto, the
rats and roaches in tenements, and inadequate schools, while
James Thomas's "Highway 61" celebrates the road which lies a
hundred feet from his Delta home and runs north to Chicago.
Rural bluesmen like himself describe isolation with stark images
like an empty room or a highway in the Mississippi countryside.

The blues come from the country, I believe. You take
long time ago, you catch fellows out in the field plowing a mule and you could hear 'em late in the evening
singing. Singing the blues. That's why I say the blues
come from the country. Just like when they be singing:

I'm setting here a thousand miles from nowhere in this one-room
country shack.

Yes, and I wonder will my baby be coming back.
I wake up every night about midnight, I just can't sleep.
All the crickets keep me company, you know the wind howling round my feet.[39]

A blues perspective emerges as Thomas speaks and sings about life in a world where:

> Rock is my pillow and cold ground is my bed.
> The highway is my home, Lord I might as well be dead.[40]

Early Sounds

Blues probably developed after the Civil War when black musicians were free to travel throughout the South and develop their repertoires. W. C. Handy and Big Bill Broonzy mention that the music was sung before 1900 and since the mobility so important to blues performers in this century was not possible before the Civil War, we can speculate that the music developed as a separate musical genre when the South moved from plantation to sharecropping economy.[41] Certainly the instrument most commonly associated with the blues—the guitar—is never seen in pre-Civil War illustrations, and unlike most early slave songs and hymns, blues are performed by solo musicians.

Slave songs similar in theme to blues were composed by musicians who voiced black suffering and used music to relieve those who had been mistreated. One former slave explained why so many of his songs dealt with suffering.

> I'll tell you, it's dis way. My master call me up, and
> order me a short peck of corn and a hundred lash. My
> friends see it, and is sorry for me. When dey come to de
> praise-meeting dat night dey sing about it. Some's very
> good singers and know how; and dey work it in—work
> it in, you know, till you get it right; and dat's de way.[42]

Just as these "very good singers" could take an experience and "work it" into a musical frame, blues singers later commented on events in their own community through their music. The blues were witness to problems of the black community.

One possible influence on early blues is Afro-American work songs like those Fanny Kemble describes in her *Journal of a Res-*

idence on a Georgia Plantation in 1838–1839. Black oarsmen
rowed her boat into a stream and:

> set up a chorus, which they continued to chant in
> unison with each other, and in time with their stroke,
> till their voices were heard no more from the distance. I
> believe I have mentioned . . . the peculiar charac-
> teristics of this veritable negro minstrelsy—how they all
> sing in unison, having never, it appears, attempted or
> heard anything like part-singing. Their voices seem of-
> tener tenor than any other quality, and the tune and
> time they keep something quite wonderful.[43]

Work songs are a common part of black culture in both West
Africa and the New World and are used to coordinate groups of
laborers. Usually one man "calls" the verses and a group works to
the tempo of his call, responding with a line of chorus after each
line or verse. Work songs are still sung by railroad workers and
by prisoners in the State Penitentiary at Parchman, Mississippi,
and parallels between verses of blues and work songs suggest the
two forms are closely related.

Before the advent of mechanized farming and construction,
black work gangs frequently used song as a means of pacing
their labor. An experienced caller set the appropriate pace for
the job and saw that work continued steadily without overtiring
his crew.

Though work chants have largely disappeared their sounds
can still be heard in Parchman State Penitentiary at Camp B,
near Lambert, where black prison gangs sing work chants as they
cut wood and hoe cotton. Their leader calls a phrase and a re-
frain is repeated by workers in a call and response pattern which
can continue indefinitely. When a tree is cut or the hoers reach
the end of a row, the caller signals the end of his chant by crying
"Mud! Mud! Mud!"[44]

Parchman work chants often speak of escape. One declares,
"Take this hammer, take it to the sergeant. Tell him I'm gone,"
and its verses describe how a prisoner "made it across" the
Sunflower River, which borders the prison, so that bloodhounds
could not follow him. As axes or hoes fall on each beat, other
verses declare love for women with names like "Rosie."

Boat up the river turning around and around.
I said her fly wheel knocking 'Bama bound.
I said her fly wheel knocking, well, 'Bama bound.

Chorus: Oh Rosie,
              Well, oh Lord Gal.
              Oh Rosie.
              Oh Lord Gal.

Said I'll cut your kindling, Gal, I'll build your fire.
I'll tote your water from that boggy biar [bayou].
Said I would do your cooking but I don't know how.

Chorus:
Said Rosie, Rosie, Gal will you be mine?
Said I won't do nothing but wash and iron.
Said gal you just do what I tell you to do.
Said I'll be true to you, you know, well true to you.

Chorus:
Said Woman, Woman, you don't know my name.
I'm the same grand rascal stole the watch and chain.
I'm the same grand rascal want to be your man.
I'm the same grand rascal used to hold your hand.

Chorus:
Well you won't write me, you won't come and see.
Say you won't write me, you won't send no word.
Said I get my news from the mocking bird.
Said I get my news from that mocking bird.
"Mud! Mud! Mud!"[45]

Work chants also direct railroad crews who line heavy steel tracks. When workers lift tracks a caller directs their moves. Railroad construction has specialized jobs, and a caller on the "Tamping Crew" uses chants which would not be appropriate for the "line crew" which lays rails. The weight of steel tracks makes it essential that every man work together. An individual's failure to do so places more strain on the rest of the crew or, even worse, may cause a fatal accident. Cal Taylor led work crews in the Mississippi Delta for fifty years and explains how on each beat the crew slowly moved heavy rails into position:

When you're lining track you say:

> Oh, up and down the road I go,
> skipping and diving for my forty-four.
> Ha ha, way over.
> Ha ha, way over.
> Poor boys, pull together.
> Track'll line much better.
> Whoa!

Then we might say for the next track:

> Oh, I got a letter from Haggis Town.
> East St. Louis was burning down.
> Ha ha, way over.
> Ha ha, way over.
> Poor boys, pull together.
> Track'll line much better.
> Whoa!

There's a lot more verses for track lining, but most of 'em got bad stuff in 'em. If you don't care I'll put them on there too.

> Oh, talking about a pretty girl, you oughta see mine.
> Great big titties and a broad behind.
> Ha ha, way over.
> Ha ha, way over.
> Poor boys, pull together.
> Track'll line much better.
> Whoa![46]

Work songs and blues are closely related in composition and theme. The chanter and the blues singer both use familiar verses which they insert at will until either work or dance is completed. The flexible form of work chants is easily transferred to the blues, where singers often vary the length of a song according to audience response. Escape from oppressive labor and love for women are developed as themes in both and strongly suggest work chants fathered the blues.

As work chants are sung, call and response maintain a constant link between the individual singer and laborers. The singer leads workers with an appropriate tempo and his musical direction is respected by both the gang and their overseer. Because callers usually do no manual labor and are paid higher wages than other workers, their music becomes a means of escaping manual labor. Broonzy emphasizes that he and his brother avoided heavy work in fields through their singing:

> So we both [he and his brother] went back to playing and we was the best two Negro musicians around there. That's what the white people said. We would be playing and sitting under the screened porches while the other Negroes had to work in the hot sun and the white people called us 'their Negroes' and thought we was too good to work with the other Negroes.[47]

Broonzy recalled well-known blues players known as "sweet back papas" who prided themselves in making a living from their music and the gifts of women admirers.

> These big-town blues players. . . . They lived like a king because most of them had women cooking for some rich white man, and they lived in the servant's house behind the white man's house.
>
> These musicians was not seen in the day. They came out at night. His meal was brought out to him from the white man's house in a pan by his woman. We called them kind of men "sweet back papas."
>
> Them men didn't know how cotton and corn and rice was grown and they didn't care. They went out, dressed

up every night and some of them had three and four
women. One fed him and the other bought his clothes
and shoes. These is the men that wear ten-dollar Stet-
son hats and twenty-dollar gold pieces at their watch
and diamonds in their teeth and on their fingers.[48]

For some bluesmen like Broonzy, musical ability was a way of
avoiding heavy manual labor, which was the fate of most blacks
in the rural South.

The mobility of singers helps explain how blues spread
throughout the Deep South by the beginning of the twentieth
century. Blues such as "Joe Turner," for example, were part of
the repertoire of Big Bill Broonzy's uncle before 1900, and W. C.
Handy heard blues in Tutwiler, Mississippi, in 1903.[49]

Since that time Mississippi Delta blues have been extensively
recorded by folklorists and on popular "race records," and these
recordings offer an important historical perspective on the sound
of contemporary singers.[50] On these recordings the Delta blues
style is characterized by a heavy sound and rough intensity. The
vocal tone is "produced at the back of the throat with rougher
growling tones, and the falsetto voice used for contrast or emotional emphasis."[51] Handy's description of the lone singer he met
in Tutwiler suggests the power of early Delta blues.

A lean, loose-jointed Negro had commenced plunking a
guitar beside me while I slept. His clothes were rags;
his feet peeped out of his shoes. His face had on it some
of the sadness of the ages. As he played, he pressed a
knife on the strings of the guitar in a manner popu-
larized by Hawaiian guitarists who used steel bars. His
song, too, struck me instantly.

Goin' where the Southern cross the Dog

The singer repeated the line three times, accompanying
himself on the guitar with the weirdest music I had
ever heard. The tune stayed in my mind.[52]

Learning the Blues

Many Mississippi blues singers began to play music with a homemade instrument known by some as a "one-strand on the wall." Children who could not afford a guitar took a wire from the handle of a broom and stretched it on the wall of their home. A hard object such as a stone raised and stretched the wire at each end to its proper tone, and as one hand plucked a beat, the other slid a bottle along its surface to change the tone. The result was a haunting sound which strongly influenced the blues style known as "bottleneck" guitar.

One-stringed instruments are common in both West Africa and Brazil, and Mississippi examples are usually nailed on the wall of a home which serves as a resonator for the instrument.[53] Sometimes groups of musicians string several wires on the same wall and play in unison for dancers. As a child, B. B. King built and played a one-strand.

I guess that was kind of like a normal thing for the average kid to do because instruments wasn't very plentiful in the area where I grew up. When we felt a need for music, we'd put the wire up. We usually would nail it up on the back porch. Take a broom wire.

They had a kind of straight wire wrapped around that straw that would keep this broom together. So we'd find an old broom or a new one if we could get it without anybody catching us. You'd take that wire off of it and you'd nail that on a board or on the back porch.

Once you nailed this nail in there, put that wire

around these two nails, like one on this end and one on the other and wrap it tight. Then you'd take a couple of bricks and you'd put one under this side and one under that one that would stretch this wire and make it tighter. And you'd keep pushing that brick, stretching this wire making it tight until it would sound like one string on the guitar. Like that.[54]

Louis Dotson has played the one-strand for fifty years and nails his instrument to his home's front wall. He compares his house to a guitar body in that both serve as a resonator.

When you put it up side the wall, it'll play. I'd say the house must give a sound to it. Just like a guitar.

When I started I didn't have no radio and I had to have some music some kind of way. So I put me up a one-strand and made my own music.

The way I decided to do, I said I'll put me a brick and a staple up there at the top and one at the bottom to pull it tight, just as tight as I can git it.

The brick at the bottom, that's where you git your tightening, from the bottom. Knock it down till you git it real tight. When you git it real tight, you go to picking and she'll play good then.[55]

When a guitar could be found, aspiring musicians often played it secretly when its owner was not around. The young musician listened carefully to older performers and imitated their notes and chords. James Thomas talked about how he began to play blues on his uncle's instrument.

I learned from my uncle. He showed me two or three chords and he would charge me to play his guitar. But after he'd leave home his wife would let me play and I didn't have to pay nothing.

I'd play till noon when he come in for dinner. Then at one o'clock he'd go back to work and I'd play till night. That's how I began to learn how.

Then after I learnt I used to go and play for dances

with my uncle. He'd pay me a dollar a night. Oh, I had
a hard time learning. I've got some work tied up in it.

Instruments were so high that it was a long time before I could get an electric guitar. When you're playing
for a big crowd of people you needs an electric guitar
because with a regular guitar you've got to work too
hard. The electric is to help you out and give you more
rest so you don't have to play so hard.[56]

The evolution from one-strand to standard guitar to electric guitar
was a familiar pattern in many communities. Musicians began
with the simplest instrument, later acquired standard and electric guitars, and the early sound of the one-strand endured as
these six-string instruments were played in a "bottleneck" style.
Using an "open" turning the musician often slides his bottleneck
along one string just as the bottle had been used on the one-
strand. Elmore James, the acknowledged master of bottleneck
blues, first played on a one-strand and James Thomas began his
blues career by secretly playing with him. Thomas explained:

I wasn't allowed at night clubs but I would slip out on a
Saturday night, and Elmore James played all night
long. That was north of Yazoo City on 49 East.

I'd slip down there and play with Elmore and Sonny
Boy Williams. Sonny Boy Williams, he didn't like me to
play Elmore's guitar, but Elmore, he didn't care. He'd
let me play long as I'd want to, and Sonny Boy would
set on the stage and roll his eyes.[57]

Talking the Blues

When performers explain the blues they often become emotional and are deeply moved by memories associated with their music. They sing of pain and suffering, and definitions of the music must begin with these feelings. Bluesmen "talk the blues" with the power and eloquence of their music, for both spoken and sung performances describe the same emotional core. Blues speech comments on the black man's condition and shows how the artist studies his people and voices their experiences. As in the music, his audience responds to the impact of blues narrative with comments like "Yeah," "That's right," and "Tell it like it is."

> The reason why it's here is a bunch of us like blues. We study that. That's all we can do. We never had no money or nothing. What else we gonner study 'bout but something to have a good time with? So that's why these blues come from us. We never had no money. We never had no place to go and have a nice time. We work all the time, so we try to git us a old guitar.
>
> Gimme a bucket and let me knock here and show him how it go. We have a good time. Take a washboard, take a comb with paper. Sometimes we have a guitar. Sometimes we have a broom. [Blows on comb.][58]

* * * * *

Why do you think they play the blues in Mississippi? Because of the way they used to plow the folks here, chop cotton at daylight in the morning. They would get

out there and work so hard, they be even looking at the
sun, saying, "Hurry, hurry, sundown. Let tomorrow
shine."

They wanted the sun to go down so they could stop
working, they worked so hard. They learned the blues
from that. And then they learned the blues from the
women. You can get the blues about a woman, you go
to kissing and hugging her, and then don't get to see
her for three or four nights. You can get the blues there.

Understand me now? You touch one up light and you
won't see her three or four days, that will give you the
blues. Most anything like that will give you the blues.
And Mississippi got more of it than anywhere 'cause all
the blues people come up here singing the blues.[59]

❋   ❋   ❋   ❋   ❋

Everything here is the blues. It goes back to feelings.
How you feel today. You know blues has always been
something that you don't have to be black to have the
blues. You can be white and wake up in the morning
and something is blue on you. You understand what
I'm talking about, around your bed, and you done got
blue.

So you understand what I'm talking about. Everybody gets the blues sometime or another. I know you've
had the blues. I'm sure you've had the blues sometime
or another in your life. Like when your girlfriend quit
you. You thought you was in love and she was in love,
and all at once you found out she's gone and you say,
"Man, I'm sad here, and I'm blue."

That's what it is. Uh Huh. Everybody get the blues. If
you wake up in the morning and don't have no money
in your pockets, and you can't get a loaf of bread, ain't
you blue? And the baby crying too!

Now I'm going to tell you about the life of the blues.
Now this is the blues:

Living ain't easy and times are tough.
Money is scarce, we all can't git enough.

Now my insurance is lapsed and my food is low.
And the landlord is knocking at my door.
Last night I dreamed I died.
The undertaker came to take me for a ride.
I couldn't afford a casket,
And embalming was so high,
I got up from my sick bed because I was too poor to die.
Now ain't that blue?[60]

Blues Generations

Blues records are generally appreciated by adults in their thirties and older. The younger generation in the Delta has turned from blues to soul music, and teen-age phrases like "soul brother" and "soul sister" reflect their new attitudes. Young people associate blues with black accommodation and feel the music is inconsistent with their life-style. When we approach blues we must understand they are the expression of a generation which grew up before the Civil Rights Movement, and attitudes expressed in their verses are very different from those of "soul" singers like James Brown and Aretha Franklin.[61]

James Thomas's daughter, Earlie Mae, prefers soul music to her father's blues, which sound dated to her ears.

> I'm not just talking about my daddy's music, but it's *old folk's* music. That's the way I feel about it. Soul music is more popular and that's mostly what the teen-agers dig. The old folks dig blues to dance off but I can't.[62]

As music styles evolve, so do the dances which they accompany. The most common dance done with country blues was the "slow drag," sometimes called the "snake hip." Young people are now on "fast time" and want to "swing out." Thomas comments how instead of embracing in a slow drag, partners move apart on a fast beat.

> When I play at a Saturday night dance they always want to do the slow drag. Some calls it the snake hip.

> But now the young people are all on fast time. They
> swing out. The one you dance with is over there and
> you way over here.[63]

Younger people in Leland who want a fast beat go to Jones
Cafe, where dances have names like "hook it to the mule." Earlie
Mae explains the scene.

> It's all my age and over. It ranges from about thirteen
> until about thirty-five. Something like that. We "hook it
> to the mule" and we "social." All the new dances.[64]

The present division between blues and soul music is not the
first such musical shift which has appeared in the Delta. Blues
singers recall older performers who sang before their era in
styles that became dated. Serious musicians recognize their debt
to these older singers who created a base from which they developed their own blues. Though younger singers create variations
on older styles, the influence of past musicians is always felt.
B. B. King, for example, acknowledges that his blues stand on a
"foundation" built by earlier singers.

> I think that young musicians have a groundwork laid
> for them. The older ones have left something for you to
> build on so you build your own ideas upon that founda-
> tion, on top of what has already been built.
> I used to hear Blind Lemon, Lonnie Johnson, and
> quite a few of the older blues singers. That was *real*
> blues to me. I think most of us that started after listen-
> ing to guys like Lonnie Johnson and Blind Lemon and
> maybe Big Joe Williams. Quite a few of the guys like
> that, we had to kind of come by them. We couldn't just
> start a new thing all of our own and not learn some of
> the old songs that they did way back.
> A lot of old blues go way back. Each generation puts
> its own thing to it and makes it sound a little different.
> But the roots are still right there and you can still feel it
> when you play.[65]

Arthur Lee Williams, a blues harmonica player near Birdie, recalls "Cross Cut," an old musician who could not play the style in vogue when Williams began to perform. In spite of this difference, Williams and other young musicians accepted the old man in their group and allowed him to perform out of respect for his tradition. Cross Cut played the bottleneck style using a case knife for his slide.

> I knew a fellow that played in that style once. He was all crippled up and couldn't walk, but that cat was out of sight with a case knife. He'd take a regular old kitchen knife and twist it up in his fingers some kind of way, and he was bad with a guitar. They called him "Cross Cut" and he had some chords that was out of sight. He was an old fellow. I imagine when he died, he was about seventy. He was a tough old man, but he fought that whiskey and them late hours and drank heavily. He was a good guitar player in his style. At that time we had stepped out of that bracket.
>
> Him being as old as he was, that made us a little different in style, you know. We would cut a'loose and let him play what he wanted to play. He played all the real old stuff.[66]

Williams comments on his relationship to the new soul sound in music and feels the division between his style and that of soul singers is comparable to the generational difference discussed above. He stresses that each generation of blacks has its own "soul" music and few singers can appeal to both young and old.

> Take James Brown, I don't care nothing about that. I listen to it, but as far as gitting a lot of feeling out of it like a lot of people do, I just don't have no feeling for that kind of music. I'd rather set down and listen to me some nice soft blues. I'd rather listen at that than to hear all that loud hollering and screaming stuff. It's just more soulful to me.
>
> See, it's a altogether new set coming along now. Just like it was between me and this old guy I was telling

you about. He played a nice style of music, but it was old to me. Just like my style of music is old to these kids now. They like James Brown and Wilson Pickett and O. V. Wright and all like that.[67]

Singers trained in one blues style can rarely break away and play for new tastes, and for this reason most blues singers appeal primarily to listeners of their own generation. Older blacks turn to blues to recall lost love and deal with their feelings of suffering and depression. Through the blues, memories return as a message or truth about one's life.

I think the blues came from people who felt bad. They sung what they felt. This was in a era when they had no other way of expressing their emotions really. They might lose their wife, their wife walk off and leave them and they'd sing about this. They felt like if their wife heard them on a record she might come back. This was their means to git the message over that they really felt bad about it. They'd let the whole world know about it.

The people that's really singing old-time blues today are people who basically came from that generation. Not necessarily them, but their ancestors did, and this has rubbed off on them through time and tradition. You find most of the people who sing these blueses are thirty-five, forty, or forty-five-year-old men, see, who have actually lived in that period.[68]

These older bluesmen who traveled and sang along found it difficult to coordinate their music with contemporary blues bands. As blues bands evolved, they were forced either to adapt their music to a group or to continue performing alone. Many of the "old heads" refused to rehearse with other musicians where they had to change their timing to suit the group.

These old heads is set in a groove and they can't get outta there. I noted that about a lot of guys. They have a certain style and even if they play another number, you can still hear that old style in there. You git some of them same old guys you got recorded there [traditional blues performers] and try to git them to do some of the new stuff. If they can do it, I bet you can still hear some of that old stuff that they put on first. It's in there and they just can't git outta that.

These old guys, they just didn't never play with anybody. They played by themselves all the time, or either with just a two-piece. Just like you had a harmonica and a guitar, that's all he'd hear. At that time there really wasn't any bands, and these guys would just git together where they had good cold beer and a little whiskey and they'd just set there and enjoy themselves. But if you put these guys with a five- or six-piece band, they wouldn't know what to do or where to start at.

Your man, Pine Top [piano player at the Blues House Party], we had him down on the organ, and he was gone, man. He didn't leave any space in there for the others to play. He was playing all the parts. He didn't give the harmonica a chance to play, and he'd cut us off during the solos, if you did sneak one in. That's no practice. That's all I can say. I used to do it before I started practicing. I had some good sounds, but I didn't have the time. I knowed I had a tough sound, but I learned how to follow the time. It took me two years to straighten that out.[69]

Unlike Cross Cut and Pine Top, young musicians worked to change their style from solo blues to a band sound. Williams practiced harmonica regularly with his group to learn their timing and feels rehearsals were a key to his success.

When James Thomas moved to Leland he also adapted his guitar style to a blues band sound. Once the change was made Thomas found he could play a more elaborate lead melody while a second guitarist played the base line. The band maintained a constant rhythmic background and freed him to experiment instrumentally. For both Thomas and Williams the key to joining a blues band was learning to "play better time." A solo guitarist may shift stanza patterns at will, but when he joins a band he has to respect a common beat and work within its frame.

When I first come to Leland I couldn't hardly play with none of the fellows around here because I always played by myself. I always played my lead and bass together on one guitar by myself. After I got here and played with the boys, that caused me to play nothing but lead or bass. That makes it easier on you, and you can play better time. A lot of records they making today, you can't play lead and bass by yourself because your lead is way down on the guitar and your bass is way up in A flat somewhere.[70]

Records

Records increased the distance between blues generations because a singer either played the new recorded sounds or continued playing in the same "groove." And no matter how versatile, the solo performer could never match the sound of blues bands which featured several guitars, a harmonica, and drums together. Even the separate bass and lead guitar melodies became too complicated for a lone guitarist. The musician was thus forced by records to abandon solo performances and join a band to give listeners the latest blues sounds.

To expand their repertoire performers borrow verses from both contemporary and older recordings. They rework these verses to suit their own needs and usually do not imitate the entire recorded version. James Thomas stresses how "You have to git verses out of records. You can git a verse out of each record and make you a recording of your own." Records are thus an important source of verses as well as melodies and guitar styles which Thomas inserts in his own blues tunes.

> A lot of the stuff that come, you never can git it just like
> the record, but you can git close to it. When you start
> to playing you can put it over to the people and they
> know what you doing.[71]

Many Delta singers feel that in order to break into the recording industry they must "base" their style on popular blues artists. A singer therefore listens to records by his favorite bluesman and reworks the material to develop a similar sound. James Thomas told me he wants to "fall in the place" of either Arthur "Big Boy"

Crudup or Elmore James. They are closest to his own style, and
by imitating them he may make a successful recording. Thomas
sang the following blues and then explained how he took it from
a record by Crudup.

> Ethel Mae, Ethel Mae,
> Darling, what are you trying to do?
> Ethel Mae, Ethel Mae,
> Darling, what are you trying to do?
> You know well I love you.
> Why don't you let me be?
>
> You's my all-day study,
> You is my midnight dream.
> You's my all-night study,
> You is my midnight dream.
> And I wonder, Lord, I wonder,
> What is this woman done done to me.[72]

> Now that's "Big Boy" Crudup, Arthur "Big Boy" Cru-
> dup. I think he's out of Chicago, but he must be dead
> now because he ain't recorded. When I start recording,
> I'm gonner fall in his place or either Elmore James. I
> like their style.[73]

Arthur Lee Williams made a similar statement regarding his
own blues style. He plays blues harmonica and patterns his performances after records by Little Walter and Sonny Boy Williamson. He told me, "I likes Little Walter's style. I kicked off
with Little Walter and then I ended up with a mixture of Little
Walter and Sonny Boy Williamson too."

Delta blues musicians are heavily influenced by records and
use the term "record" when referring to blues tunes previously
recorded. Musicians also use "record" as a general term to indicate any blues song, including those they compose themselves.
Records supply a large body of verses which circulate among
Delta singers and help mold the styles of singers as they imitate
their favorite blues performer. "Imitation" is used with care here,
for extensive changes in instrumental accompaniment and verses

reflect the singer's own taste and make the song as much his creation as that of the recorded performer.

The blues audience also identifies with familiar records which help to "consolate" their minds when they are depressed. Whatever their feeling, a blues record speaks to it. Often even popular artists base their sound on traditional blues forms such as the twelve-bar verse.

> I know myself, right now I gits worried and maybe I git worried here at the house. Well, I git up there and I play me a record. I play me a couple of records, and it look like it give me ease.
>
> You know just about every new song that come out, if you listen to them close, you'll find they have the same pattern, the same twelve-bar blues pattern. But you can modify it and turn it around if you add a little to it or take a little from it. You take James Brown, he's one of the hottest Negro artists going and just about everything he plays is based around a twelve-bar blues. It's very hard to get away from the twelve-bar pattern.[74]

Records thus influence Delta blues on two levels. First, contemporary recording styles are imitated by Delta performers, who hope they will lead to recording success, and secondly, singers "update" old records and introduce their lyrics and music in their repertoire.

Musicians update an old record for contemporary taste by rearranging its tune around the same verses. Frank Frost plays guitar and harmonica with a group in Lula and explains how he takes old "cotton-picking" blues and adapts them for local dances.

> I take them and rearrange them, and it be a new recording to them. In other words, we taking the down blues and bring it up tempo. I don't know what you would call it. Just take the cotton-picking blues, I would say, and bring it up to modern music today. I guess that still be blues.
>
> The onliest difference between the cotton-picking

blues and what we doing today is the tempo. We using practically the same words. Maybe one word in the whole thing will be changed. Let me see if I can give you something to remind you of back in those days.

Now that's just the old ordinary original way, you know. That's just the cotton-picking blues that way. Then we change up just the tempo and the beat. That's the dance tempo you hear now.

Just something they can dance to these days. That's the same blues. We just change the beat. It's no different.[75]

II   BLUES COMPOSITION

You sit down and hum to yourself. You try to see if that fits and if that don't work, you hum you something else. And then too you may pick out a verse from some other song and switch it around a little bit.

Arthur Lee Williams, Birdie, Miss.

The flexible structure of blues allows for considerable reworking of verses by singers, and a bluesman's version of a particular song is considered his own even when he admits he learned it in a different form from another singer. Many blues singers in fact claim authorship of well-known ballads such as "John Henry."

This claim of authorship based on revision of verses and singing style was explained to me by Sonny Matthews, a musician who quit singing blues when he entered the church and now sings only gospels. I asked him if he learned his songs from others and he replied:

I'll hear somebody else sing it and then I'll put my words like I want them in there. This song was by Reverend McGee at Drew, Mississippi. I was at his church and I heard him sing that. But now he sing it a little different from what I do. I just sing it in my voice and put the words in there like I want them.

Them my words there. I spaced them words like that on a contention that so many peoples singing alike, till you know that's just about to put a ruination on the gospel singing in this part. So many peoples is trying to imitate other folks, you know. They trying to mock other

songsters. I will sing their songs, but I will put the
words my way. If he have a word go one way, I'll
change it and put it another. That's the way I do most
of my singing.[1]

Like those gospel songs, the blues are reworked by singers
who structure verses according to their own taste. In this sense a
singer can justly refer to a song as "my own" because he has developed a version which is unlike those used by others.

Delta blues are sung primarily in jook joints and house parties,
and their length depends partly on the enthusiasm of dancers.
Audience response can determine whether a song is terminated
after several stanzas or continues indefinitely. This flexibility of
blues is due to verses which the singer adds to appropriate tunes
when the audience encourages him to continue. For example,
when James Thomas inserts verses in a song to prolong it for
dancers, he matches verses with similar stanzaic pattern to tunes
with a corresponding "time."

Nowdays, you git to playing and as long as the people
is enjoying the record [the song] and dancing, they
plays on it. You just keep a'playing. You have to get
verses out of records. You can git a verse out of each
record and make you a recording of your own.

That's something else I can do. If I'm playing and
don't know the song, I can add verses as I play. It
comes to me, the right verses of what to say and everything. I can make them match with the music, and
bring it in time.

Just like if you were gonner make up a song about
Vicksburg. Now you heard about the song they made
up a long time ago about "Vicksburg on the high hill
and Jackson just below." Well now, that fellow, he was
making that by head, you see. He skipped way over
from Jackson to Vicksburg.[2]

Thomas stresses that records are an important source of verses
for blues singers. Most recorded blues singers were folk rather
than popular performers, and their materials are easily assimi-

ROOTS

Shotgun home, Waltersville.

Cotton field, Parchman Penitentiary.

Louis Dotson plays his one-strand on the wall.

Plucking the one-strand.

Interior wall of Louis Dotson home.

Cal Taylor, railroad chanter. Lula.

Lula.

Work chants, Parchman Penitentiary.

KENT'S ALLEY

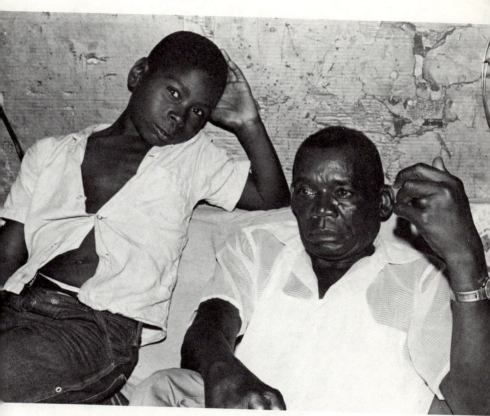

Shelby "Poppa Jazz" Brown and his son, Johnny.

Fireplace in Poppa Jazz's home. (The skull and birds on the mantel are made by James Thomas.)

lated into the repertoires of other Delta singers. Thus, as Thomas said, a singer might take verses from several records and incorporate them all into a single blues performance which then becomes "his" song. Though verses are often borrowed from other singers or from records, the over-all arrangement is his own.

Blues singers cannot simply imitate a record when dances continue longer than the three or four minutes allowed in recording sessions. To prolong the dance the performer relies on his memory to supply verses which fit the tune. A singer with a limited repertoire of verses may introduce the same verses into several songs during the course of an evening, but the gifted performer has extensive recall of verses and may play for hours without repeating himself.[3]

As the bluesman sings, he shifts verses and may even close with the same verse which opened the tune in an earlier performance. The close of a blues is signaled by an instrumental rather than a vocal phrase. After singing the final verse, the lead musician strikes a short phrase on his instrument which is understood as the concluding musical signature. Accompanying musicians sometimes join the lead instrument in the final notes.

Make Ups

Though most blues verses used today in the Delta are not original, singers pride themselves on being able to create verses spontaneously. These blues are called "make ups" and are set in standard verse forms. They may develop traditional themes such as lost love or publicly address dancers before others present. James Thomas explains how the theme of lost love can be integrated in a blues verse.

Just like if you have a girlfriend or wife and put a record out about them, which it is some out like that, about "When my first wife quit me and put me out on the road." Well that "out on the road" means that's out on the road looking for another one [wife]. You takes them verses and makes songs out of them. If somebody mistreats you, you can make a recording about them. See, "You mistreat me now, but you can't when I go home." That's the starting of a song and from then on you can put anything else you want after you give them the title of the record.

Just like the record come out about "Baby, please don't go." That's just like you got a wife and she packed up and gitting ready to go. That's how blues started. It ain't very many blues made that ain't made up about a woman. It's a few ain't made up about a woman, but the most of them is "My baby this" or "My baby that."

Something like "The Little Honey Bee." You ever heard the record about the "Little Honey Bee"? "Sail on, Little Honey Bee. Just keep on sailing and you'll lose your happy home." That's one of Muddy Waters' recordings. In other words he waddn't actually talking about a bee. He was talking about a woman, but he called her "My Little Honey Bee."

I can make up my own blues too. I just think of a verse and go from there. From then on you can skip around and do what you wanta do.

Just like if you blue about something and you hear a good record you like, you don't play nothing but that record. Now say if you have a girlfriend and she done gone off with some other boy, well you maybe go to the jukebox and have you some nickels in your pocket. Well it's a certain record on that jukebox gonner make you think about her. You ain't gonner play nothing but that record. That's the way that go.[4]

Thomas's final statement again stresses the importance of records. During my interviews I found that when I asked about "songs" or "blues" the singer usually assumed I meant those which had been recorded. They associated the term "song" with recorded materials and considered their own performances of little importance in comparison with recorded blues.

Though records are an important source of verses, "make ups" are commonly found among experienced blues singers, particularly when they sing in a relaxed situation and are confident that the audience is receptive to their own compositions. When I discussed make ups with Sonny Boy Watson he sang one, then explained how he composed it. He wrote the song "Rumble Go the Train" as a child and it is still part of his repertoire.

I first started playing music with what we called a "one-strand on the wall." We'd take a broom wire and we'd nail each end up and down and put a rock under it. I always put a nail between the rock and the wire so as to put a keen sound to it, you know. If I wanted to make it with a low tone, I'd slide my rock up, and if I wanted a high tone, I'd slide my rock down. Put a kind of large rock at the bottom and a small one at the top. Take me a bottle for my slide, you know, to note it with and make frets. I started that after I saw this song in a book.

Rumble go the train, rumble go the train,
Passing the field, passing the town,
Passing the tall grass turning brown.

Rumble go the train, rumble go the train,
Just see her smoking through that piney lane.

Take me back to my old home,
Take me back to my old home,
Back down in the West where the buffalo roam.

Just want see my old gal again,
Just want see my old gal again,
When she ain't got so evil, she ain't got too many men.

About that song, actually I didn't learn it. I just saw it in a first reader [first-grade reader]. I was about seven years old, I guess, and I saw it in the first reader. Somehow or other I liked it and as I growed up I thought about it more and I decided I'd make me a song out of it. So that's as far as I got with it. It was back when I was a small boy. In the first reader it looked just like it should of been the cowboys singing it because it was something about the cowboys on the ranch, you know. I could see deep in their minds just how they was doing out there. So I just thought about that all the time.

It was some pictures in the book. I remember the cowboys, and one had on a ten-gallon hat. So that didn't touch me too well. I liked that about "rumble go the train." See, he got the train and say he was going to see his Uncle Lee again. But instead of that I say I want to see my old gal again when she is not so evil and got too many men.

I'm gonner make the next song up all at once and see what I can do. Now it ain't no song. I ain't got no music or nothing to go with it. I'm gonner see what I can do from the root and branch.

Woke up this morning, all I had was gone
I looked in my bedroom, my baby had abandoned my home.

I went running down to the station, watching the train go
    rolling by.
When my baby caught the train, I just hung my head and
    cried.

She said, "Baby, tell me what it is."
When she saw me crying, she said, "Baby, that's enough. I can
    see that you're wasting your tears."[5]

In these songs, Watson creates a "make up" and composes
verses which are set in a traditional pattern. The last blues, for
instance, uses a twelve-bar verse and is a good example of how
blues are composed. The theme of lost love, the twelve-bar verse
form, and commonplace phrases such as "woke up this morning,"
"watching the train go rolling by," and "hung my head and
cried" all help establish a familiar scene for the blues audience.

James Thomas composed a make up during a dance which directs four of its six verses at Poppa Jazz, who was on the dance
floor. The dance was held in Poppa Jazz's home, and Jazz's name
is inserted in the verses in tribute to his abilities with women.
Thomas refers to him as both "Shelby Brown" and "Jazz," and in
the following text each reference to him is italicized. After the
dance, I asked Son if he could sing the verses for a second
recording, and he said he could not because they were made up
with no attempt to remember them for future performances. I
asked him what he calls this blues, and he said he had no name
for it. "That's just a make up. I couldn't necessarily go back over
that again because that's just a make up."

Once I had a girl, she waddn't but sixteen years old.
Once I had a girl, she waddn't but sixteen years old.
The first time *Shelby Brown* saw her, he tried to take her away
    from me.

What a mean woman you see, walking down the street.
She making love to most every good-looking man that she see.

No way for me to git lucky, long as *Jazz* try to hold me down.
No way for me to git lucky, long as *Jazz* try to hold me down.
But I catch *him* hanging round with that brown-skinned woman,
    gonner use him for my friend.

Some folks say them old, old worried blues ain't bad.
But that the worst old feeling, Boys, I most ever had.
[spoken] Play it, Boy. Play it. Yeah, *Jazz*.

I love my baby, my baby won't behave.
I'm gonner git me a hard-shooting pistol, gonner put her in her
    grave.

[spoken] Yeah, I git upset ever time I see her and *Jazz* do too,
    you know.
[spoken] That what make things go bad.

You can mess with my baby, but I declare you can't keep
    her long.
You can mess with my baby, but I declare you can't keep her
    long.
Because I got something there will make you leave her alone.

Minutes after this blues was sung, Eddie Quesie entered the
room and Thomas immediately greeted him through a verse.

Oh *Eddie* walked in, *he* think *he* smart.
I'm gonner tell *him* something, hurt *him* to *his* heart.
He love my baby, *he* love her for *hisself*.
She been gone twenty-four hours, seems just like a million years.
Yeah![6]

These make ups indicate the flexibility of blues in the hands of
a trained singer like James Thomas who manipulates verses with
ease to create his own materials during actual performance. The
inclusion of personal names in verses addressed to individuals in
his audience heightens the drama of Thomas's performance and
tightens his bond with dancers.

Verses

At times singers compete to see who has the most extensive verse repertoire; facing each other, they sing in alternating contest until one cannot continue.

During an all-male party one evening Joe Cooper and James Thomas began a competition with obscene verses. Cooper sang the first four verses, then he and Thomas began to exchange verses. The audience encouraged the men to sing as long as possible and the length of this blues—twenty verses—shows how verses flow into a song to lengthen its performance.[7]

Each verse is prefixed with "C" or "T" to indicate Joe Cooper or James Thomas as the singer. After the twelfth verse Cooper, who rarely sings, suddenly stops playing the guitar. Thomas asks, "Why don't you go on?" Cooper replies, "That's all I know of that one." Thomas insists he continue, and Cooper is forced to use the verse "Well tell, tell me, Baby, Baby where you been so long./ Girl, I ain't had no loving, Babe, since you been gone," which is commonplace in many blues and shows his repertoire of obscene verses appropriate for this tune is diminished.

Cooper again stops playing, and Thomas says, "Hand it [the guitar] here and let me play." He takes the guitar and continues singing for four more verses. As a seasoned performer who sings each week, Thomas could have continued with more verses if he had been pressed. His competition with Cooper shows how verses are inserted into a tune and indicates the extensive verse repertoire which an experienced blues singer can recall at will.

C. If I was swimming deep down in the sea,
   I would have all the women pulling after me.

C. Baby, you, you ain't joking, I don't care.
Well I go home with you, you let your bad man come and catch me there.

C. Yes, I went to my baby's house, and I set down on the step.
She said, "Come on, Big Man," say, "My husband just now left."

C. Yes, it's two, two more places, Baby where I want to go.
Baby, that's 'tween your legs and out your doggone back door.

T. Well, if I hit it, tell me I can git it, Baby catch me all night long.
Leave so early next morning, your real man never know.

C. I say git, git your bucket Baby, and let's go to the woods.
Well if we don't find no berries, let's make boogaloo.

T. Well, my momma, she was a seamster, well she learnt me how to sew.
Well, my daddy, he was a sawyer, and he learned me how to saw.

C. Well when I marry, now I ain't gonner buy no broom.
She got hair on her belly, gonner sweep my kitchen, dining room.

T. Well I'm gonner tell you, tell you like the catfish told the whale.
You can move your belly, but please don't move your tail.

C. Well up old gal slipped, in the nasty mud she fell.
Well I seen something, say looked just like a mussel shell.

T. I say belly, belly to belly, and skin, skin to skin.
Well it's two things working and ain't but one going in.[8]

C. Well I said toot, toot your belly, let you'n go round with mine.
Well if I can't do it, said tuck my horn way down.

* * *

T. Why don't you go on?

C. That's all I know of that one.

T. Man, play some more.

* * *

T. Well I felt her, felt her titty, and I pulled on the other thigh.
If I'd 'a felt any further believe I'd 'a fainted and died.

C. Well tell, tell me, Baby, Baby where you been so long.
Girl, I ain't had no loving, Babe, since you been gone.

T. Well I tipped, tipped to the window, yeah and I eased up the blind.
Heard my bedsprings popping, I could hear my baby crying.

C. I say git your nightgown, Baby, let your shoes in bed.
We gonner boogie woogie, Baby, till your navel turn cherry red.

* * *

T. Hand it [the guitar] here and let me play.

T. I said tease me, tease me, Woman, yeah just like I am a child.
Stop every now and then, let me know what's on your mind.

T. I say how can I, can I git it, and you keep on snatching it back?
Well I believe sometime you got Indian rubber in your back.

T. Well if I was, I was a chifforow [clothes bureau], Baby I would rumble all in your drawers.
Say, I wouldn't stop rumbling till I find your Santa, find your Santa Claus.

T. Well I asked her for her titty, or gimme her loving tongue,
She say, "Suck this, Daddy, till the goodie come."[9]

When two performers alternate in singing verses as above, both singer and audience focus on the verse as the basic unit of communication, rather than on the song as a whole. In the above blues Thomas and Cooper competed in an endurance contest of verses, and their effect could be measured by the amount of laughter which followed each verse. For example, Thomas's final verse is rarely sung and brought loud laughter from the men present because of its obscenity.

The flexibility of verses is suggested when we compare a verse in the above blues which Thomas adapted from an earlier song. Since the two blues tunes are different, he makes appropriate changes in the text so that it fits the second tune. The first version of the verse was:

Want you to tease me, Baby, just like I am a child.
Want you to tease me, Baby, just like I am a child.
I want you to stop every now and then, let me know what's on
   your mind.

Less than three minutes later in the context of a completely different song he reintroduces the verse in the form:

I said tease me, tease me, Woman, yeah just like I am a child.
Stop every now and then, let me know what's on your mind.

Blues verses are shaped by tune and differ from traditional white ballads, which follow a fixed narrative form. A few black ballads such as "John Henry" and "Stackolee" exist, but they are inappropriate at dances where the length of a song depends on audience response and the mood of the singer. Instead, the open-ended blues form offers a "complete" song which may range from five to fifteen minutes in length. A slow, down-home blues accompanies the slow drag, faster beats are played for the boogie, and the response of dancers to each influences their length.[10]

Because blues singers group verses without a narrative link, we must question two assumptions about their music. The first is that blues can be referred to by title. Record titles are usually taken from the first verse sung by its performer with the assumption that this verse will always be sung first, and that following verses have a fixed relation to it which remains unchanged with each performance. Such fixed texts are rare at dances. If musicians sing a traditional blues tune such as "Baby Please Don't Go" or the "Forty-Four Blues" often only the tune remains consistent in each performance. Though "title" identifies the tune in the minds of performers, their selection of individual verses and their order within the song will vary.[11]

The flexibility of blues verses is characteristic of Delta blues. When singers move beyond a folk context where they sing solely for dances and become recording stars their blues are less flexible, for when a popular audience requests a particular blues by name, they expect to hear the recorded version. The performer knows the record version is expected and his blues assume a fixed form when he sings in public. This form is certainly not present at Delta dances, where often only tunes remain unchanged from night to night. Thus the idea of a "title" which refers to a set text must be modified when we study blues in oral tradition.

We often equate the recording of a blues with its creation, and credit the first singer to record a song with having composed it. This view is understandable since most blues singers claim authorship of materials in their repertoire, but it is again based on the notion that the text recorded is a fixed form whose verses are composed by the singer. Such authorship is questionable in light of how blues verses circulate in oral tradition. There are certainly outstanding performers who compose verses, but we cannot determine which verses are composed and which are learned from oral tradition by a singer when we limit our study to records.

Focusing on the nature of blues verses helps us understand how a bluesman learns and transfers his music to other singers. He performs verses in contexts which place great demands on the musical creativity and memory, and the fullest expression of this skill is seen in the blues session.

Blues Proverbs

The blues verse is a tightly edited two- or three-line rhyme. Like the proverb, its terse language captures feeling with an air of finality as the first line or phrase issues a call and the second responds. A first phrase makes an initial statement and the second unveils the verse's full meaning, as when B. B. King sings:

Nobody loves me but my Momma, and she might be jiving too.[12]

or Little Milton declares:

Feel so bad, just like a ball gone on a rainy day.[13]

More contemporary verses by Joe Simon use the same unveiling technique:

> Have you ever loved somebody that don't love you?
> It bees thataway sometime.

Tight phrasing of blues verses encourages their use as proverbs, for the blues verse sums up life for both singer and audience and offers a handle for their experiences.[14] Ella Mae Callion, Tyrone Davis's aunt, finds proverbial meaning in her nephew's rhythm and blues record, "What Goes Up Must Come Down."

> That's really true. What goes up really must come down. You think about and listen to the words. You got to reap just what you sow, you know. What he's saying is what it's like. When he plays it you listen and I think you'll understand.

[Puts coin in jukebox and plays the record.]
Every day we have problems, little things. Everybody have problems, right? When he says 'What goes up must come down,' that's what it's all about.[15]

In moralizing about life, disc jockeys often use blues verses to make their points. They offer a blues line or a complete verse as a text to anchor their rap which follows. Like the Bible, blues present truth in verses which the disc jockey expounds upon in rhythmic phrases while the record plays.

In his morning program on Jackson's WOKJ Joe "Big Daddy" Louis introduces B. B. King's "Why I Sing the Blues" as his final selection. After Louis opens the song by saying, "The Man says, 'Why I sing the blues is because I live it,' his voice continues as the music plays in the background:

> I know it feels.
> When you're hurt.
> You got to tell somebody.
> Someone must understand,
> How you feel.
> The only way to do it is to say it loud and clear,
> Make sure that everyone will hear.
> It's the truth the way it is.
> That's why I sing the blues.
> This is B. B. King,
> Making a statement,
> And a natural fact.
> All you got to do is sit back,
> And dig where it's coming from.
> Listen.
> Not only with your ear, but with your heart.
> Everybody wants to know,
> "Why I sing the blues."

The music ends as Big Daddy returns to his opening line, "Why I sing the blues." Then he continues his blues talk to sign off the air.

That's B. B. King.
And that's all of our time for this morning.
And I want to thank you all for joining us.
It's been a ball.
It's been a pleasure
One that we'll treasure.
Until the next time we get together.
Maybe we'll have a better time.
But right now that's all the time.
Have a good day.
And if you're driving,
Drive carefully.
And if you're not driving,
Walk on, Baby.
We dig that too.
This is the Big Daddy.
I'll see you tomorrow.
The Good Lord willing and nothing happens until then.
Bye.[16]

Blues Conjuration

Blues singers are associated in folk tradition with Voodoo because their music, like charms, gives them special power over women.[17] When he links his music with Voodoo, the bluesman is doubly effective, and many singers actually boast of their supernatural powers. Voodoo doctors are reputed to fly through the air while invoking their spells, and in 1932 "Jelly Jaw" Short of Port Gibson surveyed his women in flight as he sang "Snake Doctor Blues":

I am a snake doctor man, gang of womens everywhere I go.
I am a snake doctor man, gang of womens standing out in the
    door.[18]

Short's reference to snakes is a Voodoo image frequently developed in blues verses. The snake or "Damballah" is a major deity in Dahomean vodun cults, and he symbolizes power in Afro-American Voodoo.[19] In blues verses he has both Voodoo and sexual associations, as in "Crawling Kingsnake Blues," where John Lee Hooker merges his identity with that of a snake.

You know I'm a crawling kingsnake and I rule my den.
I'm gonner crawl up to your window.
I'm gonner crawl up to your door.
If you got anything I want, gonner crawl up on your floor,
Cause I'm a crawling kingsnake, and I rule my den.[20]

Herbal roots are also common images in the blues and, like the snake, they carry both Voodoo and sexual allusions. The Voodoo or root doctor turns to "John the Conqueror Root," a root used for conjuring.[21] Those who understand Voodoo have a healthy respect for the root, and singers like Muddy Waters invoke its power over women in verses like:

I got a black cat bone, I got a mojo too.
I got the John the Conqueror Root, I'm gonner mess with you.
I'm gonner make you girls lead me by the hand.
Then the world will know I'm the Hoochie Koochie Man.[22]

While the root doctor conjures through herbs and roots, the blues "doctor" finds his power through music. Blues are linked with conjuration through roots in "Root Doctor Blues" recorded by Walter Davis of Grenada, Mississippi, in 1935.

The root that I'm selling, from it you get a lot of juice.
And when I'm giving it to you, Momma, you don't want to turn it loose.
I was doctoring on a woman, she said, "I can't see how it can be."
She say, "Go way from here, Doctor, you got too much root for me."[23]

In other blues verses a needle replaces the doctor's root, and sexual allusions are drawn from medical rather than voodoo tradition.[24] "Pine Top" Johnson sings of how his needle can cure a woman's "bad blood."

You got bad blood, Baby, I believe you needs a shot.
You got bad blood, I believe you needs a shot.
I said turn around here, Baby, let me see what else you got.
My needle's in you, Baby, and you seem to feel all right.
My needle's in you, Baby, and you seem to feel all right.
Now when your medicine go to coming down, I want you to hug me tight.
I'm in your pussy, put your legs up side the wall.
My needle's in you, Baby, and you seem to feel all right.
When your medicine go to coming down, Baby, I want you to hold me tight.
Bad Blues![25]

Bluesmen and Preachers

Verses sometimes shift between blues and hymns, though a strict line separates the traditions in Delta culture. Most blues singers are familiar with religious music, and at times call on the "Lord" for help with their woman. Bluesmen like James Thomas can actually transfer blues verses into a religious song if the tunes are compatible.

> You have to match the right verses. Some of them, you hear a blues start off, "Lord, I ain't seen my baby since she been gone." Well, you can turn that around. Instead of saying, "Lord, I ain't seen my baby since she been gone," you would turn around and say, "Lord, come and see about me." That the difference in it, you see.
>
> And the difference between church music and blues, the way the people's playing them now, it's no difference in the music. It's in the words, you see. You're making the same chords. Some blues you play, you could turn right around and the same blues that you play, you can play a church song on that same blues music you had over there. That's the way that works.[26]

The similarity between blues and religious music is particularly important in light of the conflict between preachers and blues singers. Both are spokesmen for their community, and their respective performances have much in common. Though sacred and secular language separates their song traditions, the preacher and blues singer deal with familiar themes of suffering

and loneliness. While one finds his solution in God, the other
turns to his love.

Sonny Matthews sings in a gospel quartet in Lula and acknowledges that many of his religious songs follow a blues beat
and key. He notes that blues singers also draw music from the
spiritual side.

> Most spiritual songs now is sung in a blues tone, and
> most of the blues made up is off of the spiritual side.
> You take the Staple Singers' "Why Am I Treated So
> Bad," they got some imitating them with a blues with
> the same tune, the same music and everything.
>
> Now Pop Staples used to play blues before he got on
> the gospel side. Most every gospel songster that's sing-
> ing once have been a blues singer.[27]

Like blues, hymns are non-narrative, and verses of both are inserted at will to extend a performance. As blues expand in response to dancers, the length of hymns varies according to the
congregation's enthusiasm. The lines of hymns echo blues as they
describe the singer's loneliness and suffering.

> I'm gonner tell my Lord when I go home,
> Bout how you treat me here.[28]

In both the manner of their composition and the stark eloquence
of their language, blues and spiritual verses develop a shared vision of black life. Musicians, in fact, describe some blues styles
as "churchy." Arthur Lee Williams, a blues harp player, feels Lee
Kizart's blues piano style has this quality.

> He pulls away from it at times, but now when he come
> to the chords, watch him. See that downbeat. That's a
> church sound right there. It really has a churchy sound
> to it, especially when he starts off.
>
> You can hear the same thing in Ray Charles's singing.
> He used to sing with a blind quarter. Did you know
> that? He did, and you can still hear it in his voice and
> the way he plays.[29]

In spite of this overlapping in style, blues performers are reluctant to "switch and play on the other side" because religious music represents an opposing view of life. Blues stress the importance of sex and at times are obscene, while religious music is strictly non-obscene and dwells on biblical themes. James Thomas, for example, separates religious and blues traditions in his mind and feels it is wrong to "cross" the two.

> If I got to church and pray and sing church songs, and then time I leave there go to a jook house and play blues, I think that's where the wrongness comes in. You ain't supposed to cross them that way. I'd be afraid to do that 'cause something bad can happen to you. That's what you call going too far wrong. You can't serve the Lord and the Devil too.[30]

Lee Kizart has played blues piano in the Delta since the 1930s and, despite Williams's description of his style as "churchy," he swears he has never played religious music. Kizart told me that he refuses to "cross up" religious and blues styles even though he may be punished after his death.[31]

> I can play spirituals, but I don't like it. I won't do like a lot of folks. Disc jockeys and things, they want you to play that mix-up rhythm, but I won't do it. I figure I got enough to give account of. You know we all got a day, but I won't cross up. I'll be punished for it. Not with you, with the good Lord above, but I won't do it [play church music]. In my day in this community they'd say, "You know that old man toting that guitar yonder, he oughta be gwine to church."

> That's what everybody said about me, you know. But now you take up the road, maybe. Ain't no maybe in it, I know what happening. In Chicago down in the basement there in the churches they got a saloon down there and every kind of hamburger and steak you want to cook, down in the basement. But upstairs they in church. No doubt it's some big reverend's place of busi-

ness. He go down and shoot himself good with some alcohol and then he go back up and serve.

But now I don't do that. I just serve one way. I won't
cross up church stuff with my stuff, 'cause you can't do
everything and be saved. I was playing with a boy that
wanted to fit my stuff in with church songs. Course you
can fit that in with church songs if you want and know
how to do it, but now I don't like that.[32]

Kizart's hostility toward religion is often voiced because blues
singers resent being called "evil" by preachers who lead lives
that are inconsistent with their own teachings. Kizart feels a
blues performer is more honorable than the hypocritical
preacher he describes because the bluesman's music openly
states the teaching by which he lives.

Churchgoers feel strongly about the sanctity of their music
and resent the use of the Lord's name in blues verses. Many are
taught from childhood that the bluesman is the "devil's preacher"
and his music symbolizes the dark side of life. When blues strike
a religious person, he should go off, sing the blues, and then ask
forgiveness. But under no circumstances should the two musics
be mixed.

Well, the difference against the blues and the spirituals,
the way I see it, they think if you singing the blues that
you sinning. And when a guy is singing a church song,
he's automatically doing something for the Lord.

After I was born my mother and father just always
taught me that the blues was sin and spirituals was
serving the Lord. They'd much rather listen to church
songs. I know my grandmother, she was the same way.
I got hit side the head a many a time for going through
the kitchen whistling something like that.

I remember a preacher said that if the blues hit him,
he would go off by hisself and then he would sing the
blues. That's to git it off his conscience. In other words
a blues singer is the devil's preacher, and if you sing
spirituals you are serving the Lord. So I would say that
is the difference between the blues and the spirituals.[33]

James "Son" Thomas.

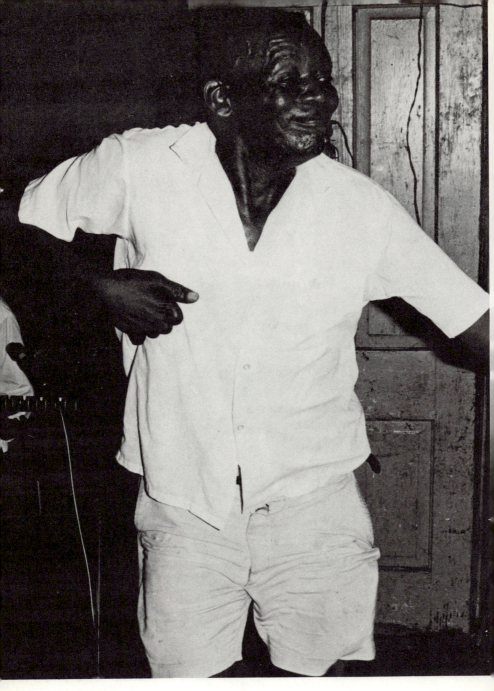

Poppa Jazz.

Talking the blues (Poppa Jazz in upper left).

Gussie Tobe sings "The Ohio River Bridge." (l. to r.) "Little Son" Jefferson, James Thomas, and Gussie Tobe. "Moonshine" seated.)

"Little Son" Jefferson slow-drags with "Juicy Fruit."

THE SANCTIFIED CHURCH AND LEE KIZART

DEAR PEOPLE LEAVE OF ALL YOUR SIN. AND REPENT. LET US TURN TO JESUS CHRIST. BEFORE IT IS TOO LATE, AND LET US CLEAVE TO GOD AND TO HIS WAY. JESUS IS THE WAY. LET US FOLLOW HIM. LET US HAVE THE LOVE OF GOD IN US TO ALL PEOPL BROTHER MINISTERS LET US COME T GATHER AND PRAY AND LET JESUS HAVE HIS WAY. TOO MENNY PEOPLE ARE GONE A STRAY. LET US CALL THE OLD AND YOUNG OUT OF THEIR SIN. MATT. 1.21 ST. JOHN 8.34.17. 3 SUN ALL ARE WEL WED NIGHT AND FRIDAY NIG

Front sign, Church of God in Christ, Clarksdale.

Interior, Church of God in Christ.

Wall behind pulpit, Church of God in Christ.

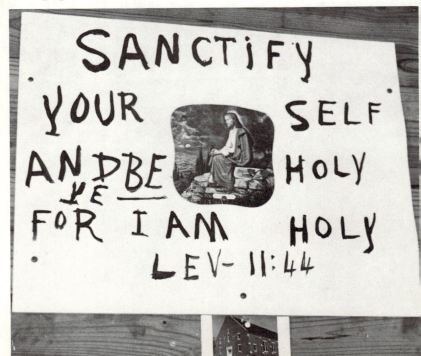

THE SANCTIFIED CHURCH AND LEE KIZART

Front sign, Church of God in Christ, Clarksdale.

Interior, Church of God in Christ.

Wall behind pulpit, Church of God in Christ.

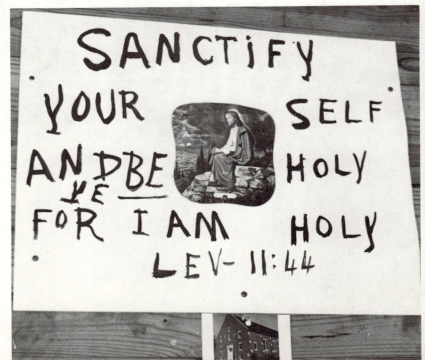

Wall of Lee Kizart home, Tutwiler.

Lee Kizart, Tutwiler.

They got a lot of verses in the blues singing about the Lord, but I don't think it's right. If you gonner serve the Lord, the Bible says you shouldn't use his name in vain. When you singing a blues song and you use a verse of the blues and then a verse of a spiritual song in there, you are doing wrong. And you're using the Lord's name in vain. When you singing a blues song, sing it straight on out and don't mix the spiritual in there.[34]

Preachers are also hostile toward the bluesman, whose music threatens their religious base in the community. Arthur Vinson feels preachers are jealous because bluesmen are better "performers" and their music is more attractive than the preaching and singing done in church.

Well, this is just my personal opinion, really. I think that your highly religious people will brand musicians that play blues and rock and roll as being "carriers of evil" for the simple reason that you can git your combo together—guitar, bass, and drums—and go out here and play. You can git up under the tree, anywhere, and the people will gather around, you see. In most cases you can draw more people out there where you're playing than the minister can draw in that church house because he's preaching and you're right across the street from him. You see what I mean. They wouldn't condone this type of music in the church.

Now if blueses had originated in the church, which it might have, as far as I know, there would not be any chaos in that line of thinking. By the same token, you take the beat, the basic beat behind your blues records you will also find behind a lot of spiritual tunes. The people git happy in church just like they'll git happy at a dance. It's the same thing. They can't dance, but they pat their feet and clap their hands and enjoy it. It's not that much difference between the types of music. It's just where you are and who you're playing for, your audience.

Then too, the words are different. Blues lyrics

wouldn't hold up in a church. You couldn't git up in a
church singing "Stormy Monday and Tuesday's just as
bad" and all that. But even in your blueses now, these
modern blueses that Bobby Blue Bland has done a lot
of, if you pay close attention to them, he calls on the
Lord. This is one of his personalized "Lord have
mercy."

In just about every one of his songs you can hear him
mention the Lord somewhere. It's not really "Lord," but
this is what they called "the Lord" a long time ago,
back in slavery times. They wouldn't say "Lord," they'd
say, "Laud, have mercy." L A U D, like that, you know.[35]

Members of the Sanctified Church are particularly odious to
blues musicians, who single out the church for criticism. The
Sanctified Church, officially termed the Church of God In Christ,
is found in larger Delta towns such as Clarksdale, Greenwood,
and Greenville, and highly charged music and religious dance are
an important part of its service. Though Sanctified Church
members sing and dance during these services, they forbid their
members from doing either outside the church and are highly
vocal in their denunciation of blues singers. Lee Kizart recalled
leaving his wife, who was Sanctified, because she criticized
blues.

I lost my wife just that way. She was Sanctified. I done a
trick when I married her. I pretended I was Sanctified
to get her. You understand. I got her and after I stayed
so long, I was out playing [blues] and I came along one
Sunday morning and she told me if that's what I had to
do, I could git my clothes and go on home. I said,
"Thank you."

I just grabbed them and packed my clothes in my
suitcase. I didn't have far to go. About as far as from
here across the railroad. They was Sanctified and they
called themselves right. So I went on and put on my
wedding shoes and I come back fixing to go out and
catch me a young pig. I had my money and stuff and
she come and told me they had got to her about it, the

Sanctified people. They said she was wrong for telling me like that, the words that she said to me. She called me to come on back home, but my clothes was down at my mother's. I said, "No. I won't go git them. You told me to take them out of here. You will be the one to go git them. I won't go git them. But I'll come back if you beg my apology."[36]

The strong emphasis on song and dance in blues and Sanctified traditions suggests why a singer can easily "cross over." For the Sancitified congregation sings and dances to an upbeat churchy sound on Sunday in much the same way the blues family celebrated Saturday night in Poppa Jazz's home.

To shift between blues and church songs reflects a choice of life-style which each person makes, and one opts for blues or religious life-styles with full knowledge of their consequences. James Thomas explains, "It's just like if you was singing the blues right now and you die, well they say you gone to hell because you was singing the blues." Those who embrace the blues and do not attend church risk this fate unless they later renounce the blues. Thomas remembers an old bluesman saying, "I'm gonner jook forty years more and then join the church." Thomas feels similarly and plans to lay his guitar aside when he joins the church lest it tempt him to return to blues. He is gradually quitting habits like gambling and drink to avoid eternity in a "sealed-up place where he can't git out."

Well, I haddn't made up my mind to join a church. I always say when I jine the church, I would lay all them blues aside. Probably quit playing the guitar, period, because if you playing spirituals and used to play blues, the next thing you know the devil git you and you gonner start right back playing the blues. I always say if I ever jine the church, I'm gonner let all that go.

I used to gamble. I quit that. I used to drink whiskey. I quit that. Now I drink all the cold beer you can git there with. I love the whiskey the best, but it make me sick and that's the reason I don't drink it. If I drink

whiskey, I can't eat nothing for two or three days. Be
weak. Can't half-work. Just make me sick.

I hear them say the devil was in heaven one time and
said the people was feeling in danger. The devil took
his tail and drug down three thirds of heaven while he
was up there. That's why the Lord put him in a sealed-
up place where he can't git out.[37]

A person chooses blues or religious life-styles as well as music.
Most blues singers attended church as children, and many
preachers frequented the blues scene before joining the church.
Blues enthusiasts and churchgoers have a common understanding in that each is familiar with the other's traditions. James
Thomas suggests the bluesman and preacher share the same
desires, but the preacher cannot express his openly.

You can't go by what the preacher say because he and
the bluesman looking for the same thing—some money,
some chicken, and a nice-looking woman. That's all
they looking for. He preaching the Bible to you but you
can't go by that.[38]

The blues scene clearly attracts even churchgoers, and bluesmen like Poppa Jazz strongly defend their life as more honest
and healthy than that offered by religion. In a tale of two
brothers, Jazz suggests that even in Hell the bluesman is hap-
pier.

Once there was two brothers. One was named Heaven
and the other was named Hell. One boy would pray all
the time and preach and the other boy what had Hell in
him would say, "Man, what you gonner do now? You
gonner always pray and ain't never gonner try to git
hold of none?"

Heaven said, "That's right, Brother. I'm on the Lord's
side. I'm gonner pray. You pray for what you want and
I'm gonner pray for what I want."

So this old boy named Hell said, "Looka here. Let me
tell you something. Now we brothers. The first one die,

that's gonner be me. Now when I die I know the devil ain't gonner let me come up from where I'm at, but the Lord will let you loose. When you die and git to Heaven, I want you to come and see me."

So sure enough the old boy died and in a few months his brother died too and went to Heaven. He went up there drinking that wine, eating that good bread. They had milk and honey and everything. So he finally thought, said, "You know, my brother told me come and see him when I die. He's in Hell and I wonder if the Lord'll let me go down to Hell and see him."

So one of the Lord's prophets was there, and he was standing listening to him. He say, "What you want?"

He say, "Reckon the Lord'll let me off and let me go down to Hell to see my brother?"

He say, "You ain't got nothing to do but go to ask him."

So he went up there and say, "Lord. Lord, come here. Would you mind letting me off for a few hours to go down to Hell to see my brother?"[39]

The Lord told him, "Yeah. But if you go down to Hell, I got to give you a length of time to come back here."

He say, "Well, all right. I'll take that chance."

He say, "Well, I'll give you until nine o'clock."

It was twelve that day. He wouldn't eat dinner. The Lord went down and he saw Jonah. Jonah standing at the gate. He said, "Jonah, give that preacher there a pair of wings and let him fly on down to see his brother. If he don't be back here by nine o'clock, don't let him in this gate no more."

Preacher say, "Well, that's all right. That's a bet, Lord."

They give him his wings, and he stretched them and flew on down to Hell. When he got to Hell, he knocked on the door. "Who is that?"

One of the devil's imps opened. He said, "This is Preacher."

"What do you want?"

"You got a boy down here named Willie. This is Preacher. This is his brother."

The imp opened the door and said, "Hey! Come on in."

The little imp started dancing around him. He come on in there. His brother saw him and said, "Lord have mercy. When did you die?"

"A few months ago."

He said, "Well come on in."

He first walked in and looked over there at a nice table where they were playing cards. He looked over there, and they was shooting dice. He said, "They allow you to do that here?"

He said, "Yeah, man. We pitches a bitch here. We pitches a bitch."

Walked up there to the bar. They had whiskey, wine, everything. He said, "Wait a minute, man. Here's where I want to stop, right here.[40]

He grabbed him a bottle of whiskey and started drinking. He turned his wings to the bar. When he turned his wings to the bar, he looked over and seed them pretty gals with hair all down here and said, "Wait a minute. Come on and let's go over here."

He went over there. [He's forgitting the time! He's forgitting the time! He had to be back in Heaven at nine.] He went on over there where them gals was and when the gal looked at him, she got up and give him a seat. He set down and she set in his lap and put her arm around him and with all that hair he knowed he was in heaven. She put that hair and them legs around him and he said, "Huh! Lord have mercy here. I ain't never had this good treatment up in Heaven."

He called his brother. "Come here, Brother. Ain't no-where I can go?"

He said, "Yeah. Just tell her."

So he whispered to her. They got up and she had her arm around him and went on up to the room where they go. He got them wings unbuckled and set 'em up 'side the bed where he could git in 'em quick. They laid there, you know, playing with one another and everything and way along about eight forty-five he said, "Huh! You know one thing, this here's a nice place."

He dozed off to sleep and when he woke up it was ten o'clock. He said, "Oh, Baby. Wait here. Look, what time is it?"

She said, "It's after ten o'clock."

He said, "Lord, I'm supposed to have been back in Heaven. I'm supposed to been back up there at nine. Wonder if they'd let me in?"

He grabbed his wings and stretched them out and flew on back to Heaven. And when he got there, he had to ring the bell. "Booo!" [Imitates bell.] Wouldn't nobody say nothing. He shook the bars. He said, "Ain't nobody in this son of a gun. They may not let me back up in Heaven."

He kept up so much noise that Jonah rode up there and said, "Who is that?"

He said, "You know who I is. I'm the man you sent to Hell on the wings."

"Who do you want to see?"

"I want to see the Lord."

"The Lord's asleep. You can't see him this time of night. He's asleep. What you want with the Lord?"

"Let me talk to the Lord. I want to talk to the Lord."

"Well, you keeping up so much noise and waking everybody up so, I'm going to get the Lord. But you can't come in."

"Just let me talk to the Lord."

So he kept worrying Jonah till Jonah went on and got the Lord and brought him up there. The Lord opened the door and said, "Preacher, what do you want?"

"Lord, I just want to let you know one thing. I brought these damn wings back to you, and I'm going back down in Hell where I belong. You can take these sons of bitches. Here they is."[41]

So he went on back to Hell. No bullshit. I ain't lying either. I ain't lying.[42]

Black and White Music

Black singers who perform regularly for whites develop a musical repertoire which is markedly different in both style and content from blues played in the black community. In 1968 James Thomas performed exclusively for black audiences around his home in Leland and had never traveled over a hundred miles from Leland.

> Clarksdale is as far north as I've played. Lexington, Mississippi, that's as far east as I've been. I hadn't did no playing over in Greenville to amount to nothing. I went over there a time or two. The furtherest south I've played is Jackson. I went there and recorded a record on Parish Street a few years ago. But the amplifier I had had a lot of static in it. That was the cause that my record didn't pass.[43]

Thomas sings some blues which are highly obscene while others deal with racial conflict in verses such as:

> The nigger and the white man playing seven up.
> The nigger beat the white man, scared to pick it up.
> He had to bottle up and go.
> Well your high-power women shore got to bottle up and go.[44]

Traditional blues have a strong racial perspective and local whites rarely appreciate what they term "nigger music." Blacks use the same phrase to stress a preference for music by their own "color."

I don't like white music at all. When I hear nigger
music, I can say that's some of my color doing that.
Sometimes I have the radio on and hear whites and
turn it off.[45]

James Thomas recorded thirty-four different songs during my
visits, and of these only one was considered "white music."
Thomas learned the piece, "Little Red Shoes," from his grandfather, Eddie Collins, who played regularly at white dances. Its
tune is played in C, a popular key for traditional white music,
and its waltz time is inappropriate for black dance steps like the
slow drag and the boogie. Though he is an accomplished blues
guitarist, Thomas plays "Little Red Shoes" with difficulty because he is not accustomed to fingering chords used in white
music. After he sang the song Thomas explained that he associates it with white "cowboy" songs rather than the blues.

> Little red shoes, my darling wore.
> Just before she died,
> She called me to the bedside.
> She willed me her little red shoes.
>
> Good bye, Little Darling, good bye.
> I hope we'll meet again.
> Willed me her little red shoes.
>
> Some day I hope we meet again.
> I hope we meet again.
> But don't you forget,
> I willed you my little red shoes.

The one I heard play that was my granddaddy, Eddie
Collins. He's dead now. He used to play for white people at dances, and that's where he got that from.

That's C natural. You play mostly cowboy songs in
that key. We call it hillbilly music, you know. Cowboy
tunes. You know before we had television we used to
tune in to the "Grand Ole Opry," and my granddaddy,

he wasn't going to miss them cowboys. I likes to learn a different tune, but don't nothing get ahead of me in the blues. I just have a feeling for the blues.[46]

Apart from "Little Red Shoes," Thomas's recorded repertoire was either composed by him or borrowed from other blues performers. Significantly, many of these other performers are Delta singers with similar styles, such as Junior Parker, Arthur "Big Boy" Crudup, Elmore James, and Robert Johnson.[47]

The White Audience

Scott Dunbar lives at Lake Mary and performs regularly for whites in a local lodge. His repertoire provides an interesting contrast with that of James Thomas. I recorded thirty-seven songs during my visits with Dunbar and of these, two thirds were sung white style in the key of C. Spirituals such as "Down by the Riverside" and "Swing Low, Sweet Chariot" also used the tempo and style of white music. Included in the body of white material were well-known songs such as "You Are My Sunshine" by Jimmie Davis, the "singing governor" of Louisiana, "Tennessee Waltz," and "Wabash Cannonball."

After he sang "Sweet Home," I asked Dunbar where he normally performs it. He replied, "What, 'Sweet Home'? Well, just like I play for that man and git something for it. It's all right if I git something for it."[48] The "man" runs a local lodge and pays Dunbar to sing for his white guests. In such a context it is clear why both the style and content of his music are heavily influenced by white musical tradition.

Mrs. Dunbar further affirmed Scott's role as a performer for white audiences and said she refuses to let him play in black jook joints because of their violence.

> We used to play for colored parties to make money but we don't go to no colored parties no more. They fight and use bad language. Right in the middle of a play they'd fight and grab their pistols and all, and I have jumped out of back doors hiding with the children many a time. They won't behave. I just quit. I said, "I

can't raise these children and carry them with all kind
of people like that." We quit. He don't play for nothing
but white people.[49]

Dunbar's songs for whites at Lake Mary contrast with
Thomas's Leland blues and show that white and black styles do
not always follow racial lines. The black musician who plays for
whites appropriately tailors his music for their taste. Though
Scott Dunbar is an extreme example in that he plays solely for
whites, I noted similar musical divisions in the repertoires of
singers who play for white and black groups.[50]

The large black population in the Delta shaped musical taste
of the area in favor of the blues. White performers from the region, such as Mose Allison, develop their own variations of the
blues sound. When live entertainment is unavailable, one can hear
the blues over local radio stations like Clarksdale's WROX or on
Nashville's powerful WLAC, where Randy's Record Shop spon-
sors a nightly rundown of the latest blues sounds colorfully intro-
duced by disc jockeys "John R." and the "Hoss Man."

Population in adjacent hills east of the Delta is largely white
and blues are rarely heard even among blacks who live there. Instead, square dances and sacred harp singing are familiar traditions among both black and white communities.[51] While the
Delta listens to blues on WLAC, people in the hills tune to
Nashville's WSM and the "Grand Ole Opry" each Saturday
night. Tom Dumas grew up in these hills near Walthall, Webster
County, and played country tunes on his fiddle for black square
dances.

> We never did go to white folks' dances, but we'd play
> for colored folks. We used to give dances about five
> nights out of every week. I played there from 1897 until
> 1904. I have sat in a corner many a night and played all
> night long. I used to pick a banjo and my daddy, he'd
> play the fiddle.[52]

Dumas moved from the Webster County hills to Tutwiler in
1922 and to his surprise found that Delta blacks had no interest
in his music. They considered his fiddle tunes "white folks'

music" and as a result Dumas gave up the music which four generations of his family had played.[53]

> This fiddle is been in the family for four generations. My daddy's granddaddy had it. That's the fiddle that Andrew Jackson had. It come from Italy, and my daddy's granddaddy bought this fiddle from Andrew Jackson, the seventh President. He learned on it and played, and my daddy's daddy learned on it and played, and my daddy learned on it and played. In 1897 I took it up and learned on it, then I stopped playing in 1904.
>
> When I come down in this country [the Delta] then, forty-five years ago, they began to come out with the talking machines, the radio. I would listen in to the "Grand Ole Opry" and the old-timey fiddle tunes, and I thought about my fiddle. I hadn't played this fiddle in forty-five years. So I went home and got this old fiddle from our barn. Rats had bored a hole and built a nest in it. It hadn't been played in about thirty-five or forty-five years. A white fellow fixed it up for me about twelve years ago, and I had to start over new like I did when I first started.
>
> I used to play for dances way yonder when I was quite a boy, fifteen or sixteen years old. I just took it up. But these here Delta folks, they don't like fiddling.[54]

III   BLUES HOUSE PARTY

Play me one of those old "road
blues" in a snuff-dipping key.

Jasper Love
Clarksdale Blues House Party

Stories, jokes, and music are all part of the blues performance.
They flow together in small rooms filled with smoke and the
smell of alcohol as couples talk, slow-drag, and sing with the performer. On summer nights their sound travels throughout Delta
neighborhoods like Kent's Alley, Black Dog, and the Brickyard.[1]

During blues sessions the audience frequently addresses the
singer and forces him to respond to their comments through his
music. A singer's life may in fact depend on how well he replies
to the verbal banter of intoxicated listeners who gather around
him. The experienced bluesman sings near a door or window
which provides a quick escape if the crowd becomes too rowdy.

James Thomas remembers one incident at a Saturday night
dance near Tchula which interrupted his music and sent dancers
running for their lives.

You take at the country dances, you get to playing the
blues and some of the women, they dip snuff. They'd
take them a big dip of snuff and say, "Yeah, you better
know your man from mine, child." You have to watch
them women dip that snuff.

I went to Tchula once. A lady wanted me to play for
her and we went northeast of Tchula, way out in the
country. So they got to fighting up there that night. A

fellow went and got some shotguns and came back and started shooting down toward the house. So that lady didn't have no husband. She got her shotgun and went out in the yard and she started shooting back at them. She ran two men away with that shotgun. Both of them had guns. I never will forget that. I never would come back there 'cause there's danger of getting shot in the face when there's a lot of people dancing and there's shooting in the house. You don't know what's going to happen. Lots of people got killed like that.[2]

Lee Kizart played blues piano in jook joints during the twenties, when the Delta was "in her bloom," and encountered similar incidents.

By myself with nothing but a good piano. By myself. That's when Ida Cox and them was on a passenger train that run through here. They called it "Teddy" with all the steel cars. Well, that was back in twenty-four and twenty-five. Then I left in the fall of twenty-six.

Along in them times this country was in her bloom. She tore up bad now. But she was in her bloom then. That's where I was. I seen many a fellow get killed at night and drug up under the skin table, but it waddn't me. I've had this door to git busted on the piano right in front of me. A woman was singing and had her hand on this door and somebody shot and busted it. Didn't bother me. I didn't git hurt. Fact of the business is, it's no more harm for me to do it than for Louis Jordan [a popular piano player of the period] and all them other big stars up there.

I seen a woman git shot one night when I was playing at a jook joint way out in the country. She had just come in from St. Louis and her head fell just about that far from the end of the porch and my car was setting right up by the porch.

Just broke her neck. It was a forty-five bullet shot all right enough. It broke her neck and she fell with her head just about that far from the edge of the porch. I

was setting down playing and I jumped out the back
door and run around to the side of the house. I got in
my car and when I cranked up, I like to drove over I
don't know how many folks up under my old racer. I
had a racer then.

They were gitting out of the way. Just like I'd of
been playing or anybody else. It waddn't none of me
did it. I was just playing for that twenty dollars. I didn't
live there. I lived in Glendora and had a cafe.[3]

In situations like these the blues singer sometimes prevents
fights by talking the blues with his audience and integrating
their conversations between his blues verses.[4] After he sings a
verse, the musician continues instrumental accompaniment and
develops a talk session. He may then sing another verse while
participants remember rhymes and short jokes which they introduce at the next verse break. The singer always controls this
talk through his instrumental accompaniment.

The following blues party is an example of how blues emerge,
verse by verse, and are skillfully manipulated by the singer to
engage his audience. The session shows the limitations of using
blues records in the study of oral tradition, for studio conditions
completely remove the performer-audience dimension of blues.
Listeners influence the length and structure of each blues performed and force the singer to integrate his song with their responses.

Records also influenced my view as a collector of blues in that
I instinctively hoped to record an uninterrupted performance of
songs. After taping several sessions it became clear that what I
first saw as "interruptions" were, in fact, the heart of the blues
performance. Experienced bluesmen read audience response as a
mark of their success, and my recordings of good blues sessions
were filled with comments and jokes told while the music
played.

I taped the following party in the shotgun home of Floyd
Thomas, which stands in a black section of Clarksdale known as
the Brickyard. The main singer, Wallace "Pine Top" Johnson, is
considered the finest piano player in the area. He learned piano

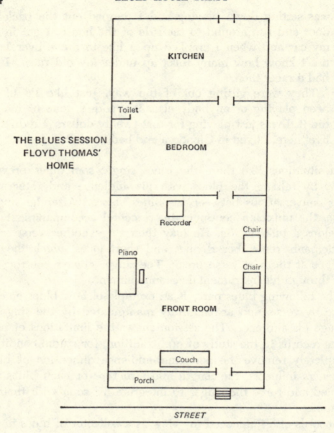

THE BLUES SESSION
FLOYD THOMAS'
HOME

KITCHEN

Toilet

BEDROOM

Recorder

Chair

Piano

Chair

FRONT ROOM

Couch

Porch

STREET

in 1933 at the age of sixteen and studied with three bluesmen, Lee Kizart, Joe Willie "Pine Top" Perkins, and "Terrible Slug."

Throughout the evening there is constant verbal interplay between the singer, Wallace "Pine Top" Johnson, and his audience, Jasper Love, Floyd Thomas, Baby Sister, and Maudie Shirley. The role of "performer" shifts repeatedly from the singer to his audience and back to the singer. For example, Jasper Love narrates the tale of a snake escaping Mississippi and an obscene joke and relates family stories learned from his grandmother. While the audience listens to Love's narration, Pine Top continues to play his piano in the background. He subtly controls the party through his music, and when tales are completed he recaptures the audience by changing his beat or striking louder chords. Pine Top shares this drama with his audience, but maintains over-all control through his music.

Pine Top carefully prepares the audience for a shift from narrative to sung performance with talk which introduces the next blues. He tells Jasper Love, "You know one thing, boy? I'm drifting." Love replies, "He's trying to drift outta Mississippi. I know what he's trying to do." Then a verse begins:

You know I'm drifting, and I'm drifting just like a ship out
    on the sea.
Well, I'm drifting and I'm drifting like a ship out on the sea.
Well, you know I ain't got nobody in this world to care for me.

Pine Top makes "Drifting Blues" an extension of his talk and shows why narrative and musical skills are both essential to the blues performer.

In songs such as "A Thousand Miles from Nowhere," verses are separated by lengthy exchanges between Pine Top and his audience throughout which he continues to play the piano. Pine Top can sing, interrupt verses while he talks with the audience, or end his performance through skillful use of verses which determine the song's length.

Blues Talk

Throughout the evening the word "talk" appears in short phrases exchanged between Pine Top and his audience, and it becomes clear that both singer and instrument talk through their music. Pine Top sings a verse, then says, "You know what I'm talking about." Later Jasper Love encourages Pine with the phrase "Talk to them, Pine." When the blues singer "talks" he communicates through his music. By playing well, he talks clearly. Pine Top sings a moving verse, and Jasper replies, "Now it's talking to me."

Within the blues performance the distinction between music and talk disappears as performer and audience respond to each other. Blues talk complements verses and at times becomes the most important part of the performance. Pine Top's long exchanges with Jasper Love and Maudie Shirley are the heart of the party. Their talk is part of a constant interplay between audience and singer which reshapes music and becomes part of his song.

Blues talk merges with verses over piano accompaniment, and sometimes Pine Top treats a long exchange as a "verse." Toward the end of the evening he sings three verses of "Hoochie Koochie Man," then talks at length with Baby Sister. He develops their talk as a closing verse which falls over piano accompaniment and ends when Pine Top sings and plays the final line of the blues, "Everybody knows I'm here."

Pine Top performs several selections twice, but exchanges with the audience in each makes them appear as "different" songs. For example, the house party opens with "Pine Top Boogie Woogie" and his music draws short comments from Jasper Love such as "I wanta hear it." In the second performance of "Pine Top Boogie Woogie" Floyd offers short comments throughout and Pine Top explains how he drove a mule before learning his blues. Pine Top's talks with Jasper Love and Floyd shape each performance into distinctly different versions.

The two performances of "One Room Country Shack" offer an even clearer example of how blues talk reshapes music. Shortly after the party begins, Pine Top plays the piece, but complains, "This piano, she's sticking on me." His performance draws only occasional comments from Jasper Love. Ten minutes later he is more comfortable with the instrument, and repeats the same song. In three important exchanges Pine Top reminisces with Jasper Love about hard work, his woman who quit him, and driving tractors for two and a half dollars a day. Their comments reshape and build a new version of the same song heard minutes before.

Two types of blues talk appear throughout the session. The first are short phrases like "Play the blues, Pine" which are tucked in the musical breaks after each line. Jasper Love is particularly adept at such short comments, and his replies are reminiscent of the blues disc jockey's style of speaking over records. Both defer to the music and lay their phrases over instrumental breaks.

A second, more lengthy blues talk develops when a speaker draws the center of attention away from the singer. At its simplest, this talk is a long conversation between singer and audience which serves as a verse within the song. The talk can also develop into obscene tales, toasts, and dozens performed with instrumental accompaniment.[5] Maudie performs each toward the end of the party while Pine Top accompanies her on his piano.

The audience is familiar with Pine Top's blues and offers leading responses to his lyrics. Pine Top sings, "I wants to know, I want to know. I just got to know," and Floyd replies, "What you want to know?" The next line answers, "Why you always play around."

In a more complicated exchange Jasper suggests a verse of "How Long Blues." While Pine Top plays, Jasper asks him, "If you should die before your time what would happen?" Pine Top replies by singing, "If I should die, die before my time, I want you to know what will become of me." Jasper then answers,

"Well, all right." Through such exchanges Jasper supports and expands on Pine Top's verses. A good example of call and response between Jasper and Pine Top develops in "Sunny Road."

I say when I was making good, you treat me like I was a king.
(Jasper) *She lied to you then.*
When I was making good, Darling, you treat me like I was a king.
(Jasper) *What happened then?*
Now you know all my money gone, and your love don't mean a thing.

Pine Top sometimes links song with talk which precedes it. Jasper tells the story of the black snake at Vicksburg, then Pine Top sings, "I got the blues for Vicksburg, Baby, sing 'em everywhere I go." Pine Top also introduces his own blues with talk when he tells Jasper, "My baby woke up early this morning and . . . told me she wanted to rock one time." Jasper replies, "Well, all right," and Pine Top sings, "Rock me, Baby, rock me all night long," as music and talk flow together in a complete blues performance.

Pine Top frequently begins instrumental sections with the phrase "Play the blues," and to credit the source of his blues he adds the singer's name, as in "Play it, Tampa Red" and "Play it, play it, Muddy Waters." Just before beginning a verse of the "Pine Top Boogie Woogie" he declares, "This is Mr. Roosevelt Sykes what's playing." Pine Top thus acknowledges his sources through talk before and after verses.

Mississippi is clearly on the blues singer's mind as Pine Top places his women in Delta towns. In "Dust My Broom" he sings, "I'm gonner find me a *Clarksdale* woman if she dumb and crippled and blind." Then later in the "Santa Fe Blues":

I say Mobile on that Southern line, *Jackson* on that Santa Fe.
You know I got a woman in *Tutwiler,* I got a woman in *Sumner* too.

Both music and talk use Mississippi as a reference point, and the singer assumes that everyone who loves blues is familiar with the state.

An important sense of direction in music and talk develops when Pine Top tells Jasper, "I'm *down* in Mississippi and I got to play the blues." His word "*down*" also has emotional associations reflected in phrases like "*down* and out." Thus when Pine Top says he is "*down* in Mississippi" he identifies both geographical and emotional states. Jasper and Pine Top make plans to move "*up*" to Chicago and escape the blues state. Jasper tells Pine Top, "I'm glad we *up* here on Seventy-ninth and Cottage Grove where we can be free . . . in Chicago, Illinois."

Jasper declares he "moved *up*" in the world by going "*out* in California." Now he has "come *back* to Mississippi to see how people are living *down* here." He places Mississippi on the "*down*" side of the blues map in both a literal and a metaphorical sense and feels that to leave Mississippi is to move up to a better life. Jasper says since he left Mississippi he has lived "with them angels. I don't do nothing now but ride a Cadillac. I'm a Mississippi boy but I done skipped from it now."

Jasper links Mississippi with sickness and death in Pine Top's blues "Going Down Slow." When Pine Top addresses his friend with the line "Love, I've had my fun if I don't git well no more," Jasper replies, "Long as you stay in Mississippi, you never will git well." Pine Top later sings of how he is slowly dying and plans to ship his body home. "On the next train south, Love, look for my clothes back home." Jasper then argues against even sending a corpse south. "You don't wanta go south. Tell him to go west or north, but don't go south."

Throughout the evening both talk and blues develop themes of escape. In their first exchange Jasper asks Pine Top, "Where you trying to make your way to?" and the response is, "I'm trying to go to California." Jasper then suggests they go south to Vicksburg because "They ain't acting right by us," and tells a tale about a black snake who was also trying to "git outta Mississippi too." Following the next blues, Jasper explains how his grandmother's generation used hymns as coded messages to escape from whites. Later Pine Top repeats his "Pine Top Boogie Woogie" and inserts the line "I'm fixing to leave Clarksdale. I'm going to California./I may go out to California." The theme of escape is woven throughout both song and talk, and finally

Jasper says, "I see you buying a ticket, man. Where you fixing to go?" Pine Top replies, "I'm going to Chicago."

Pine Top is aware of the historical setting of his blues, and when I ask him about the verse "You should of been down here in nineteen and thirty-five./The womens was quitting the mens and didn't have no place to hide," he explains it is set in the depression during Hoover's administration. He bitterly recalls, "Hoover took all the money and wouldn't feed nothing but a mule and a hog."

Movement of Delta blacks from Mississippi to Chicago is also alluded to, for both Pine Top and his audience have visited Chicago and are familiar with its streets. When Pine Top says he is going to the black community on the South Side rather than the West Side, Floyd warns him, "South Side is where they got trouble at. You better go on to the North Side." Jasper Love replies to Floyd with a blues line, "Detroit on fire and Chicago burning down," alluding to earlier racial violence in the two cities.[6]

Midway through the session Maudie Shirley enters the room and challenges Pine Top's male perspective on the blues. She introduces her own verses and replies to Pine Top's talk with phrases like "You must think I'm a fool, don't you?" and "Well, you got your womens, why can't I have my mens?" Pine Top tries to end "Running Wild" when he says, "I'm gonner finish up," but Maudie insists on her part and begins her reply with "Let me tell you one thing."

Like Jasper, Maudie is familiar with Pine Top's repertoire and at times inserts her own verses into the session. She is not, however, a seasoned performer like Pine Top and in "Running Wild" her second verse is inappropriate for the beat. She begins the verse "If you love me, Darling, I'll do anything you say" in a slow tempo which does not fit "Running Wild."

Using Pine Top's accompaniment, Maudie performs toasts, dozens, and jokes for her audience. As Pine Top addresses the audience by name in his blues line, she inserts them into her narrative.

Pine Top shapes the over-all party, beginning with his "own" song, the "Pine Top Boogie Woogie." After his third song, the audience responds with talk which occasionally occupies equal time with the songs. Pine Top responds to audience talk and skillfully integrates it with music to provide a background for the speakers. Interruptions by the audience are embraced by Pine Top through his musical response, as performer and audience merge in a total blues drama which, like the old hymns Jasper describes, "pitches sound backwards and forwards."

Pine Top is the main speaker and singer throughout the house party, and when speakers interact they are indicated with the following initials:

> P:=Pine Top
> J:=Jasper Love
> M:=Maudie Shirley
> F:=Floyd Thomas
> BS:=Baby Sister

Blues talk is underlined to distinguish it from verses which Pine Top and Maudie Shirley sing, and the end of each performance is marked with the symbol ⚹⚹⚹.

Before taping this house party I recorded Jasper Love's reflections on blues and black life in the Delta for a week. Jasper played blues piano for me several times, but insisted I meet Pine Top, who he said was the best in Clarksdale. One evening after dinner we drove to a cafe near the brickyard and found Pine Top with several friends on their way to a piano in the home of Floyd Thomas.

Floyd's upright piano stood in the front room of his shotgun house. All windows were open and a large fan pushed a breeze through the room. I had several six-packs of beer, and we each opened a can while Pine Top struck chords on the piano. Photographs of Sam Cooke and Floyd's parents hung on the wall beside a funeral home calendar and his diploma from a Clarksdale manual training school.

When the music began, several people drifted in from the street to listen, and toward the end of the evening ten people were gathered in the small room. At times an individual would rise to deliver a joke or dance to Pine Top's music.

House parties like this one are common in the Delta and happen whenever a musician finds an audience and a comfortable room to play in. Floyd's party was a more limited gathering than others I recorded at jook joints or in larger homes like that of Poppa Jazz. I selected this recording because the flow of blues, jokes, and audience response is representative and clearly audible for all voices.

The party lasted over three hours and ended after midnight when we walked Maudie back to her home and played my tapes for her children.

The House Party

P: *I'm gonner play that "Pine Top Boogie Woogie" first.*
Now look, let me tell you something about that "Pine Top
Boogie Woogie."
J: *I wanta hear it.*
Now when I say stop, I mean stop.
J: *That means it's good to you.*
I say git it, I mean git it.
Do like I tell you.
I say hold it, I mean hold it.
That's what I'm talking about.
Now, Red [Jasper Love], hold yourself.
Don't move a peg.
Now git it.
Now boogie.
J: *Don't forgit to break down that bass.*
Now look. You see that woman with her red dress on?
J: *I shore do, Pine.*
I want you to swing her right on back to me.
J: *No, I'm gonner keep her for myself.*
Don't forgit it.
J: *Aw, naw.*
I say hold it, I mean hold it.
That's what I'm talking about.
Now boogie.
Now, Red, hold yourself again.
Don't move a peg.
Now git it, boogie.
Now shake it.[7]

###

P: *I'm gonner try some more blues.*
J: *Play it like you was playing it when you was plowing them
mules.*
Now tell me, Little Girl, where you stay last night.
It ain't none of your business, you know you ain't treating me
right.
But that's all right.
I know you in love with another man, but that's all right.
Every now and then I wonder who been loving you tonight.

Now look here, Baby, see what you done done.
You done made me love you, now your man done come.
But that's all right.
I know you in love with another man, but that's all right.
Every now and then I wonder who loving you tonight.

I say tell me, Little Woman, where you stay last night.
It ain't none of your business, you ain't treating me right.
But that's all right.
I know you in love with another man, but that's all right.
Every now and then I wonder who loving you tonight.

J: *I'm gonner go git me a pint of corn whiskey 'cause I'm thirsty.*
I got a great big woman, you know, got a little woman too.
Ain't gonner tell my big woman what my little woman do.
But that's all right.
I'm in love with another woman, but that's all right.
Every now and then I wonder who been loving you tonight.
Let's go. Shake it on out.[8]

###

Well now I walked all night long, my forty-four in my hand.
Now I walked all night long, forty-four in my hand.
You know I was looking for my other woman, been out with an-
other man.
I done wore my forty-four so long, till it made my shoulder sore.

Now if I git you where I want you, Baby, ain't gonner wear my forty-four no more.

It won't be the first time that forty-four blow.
Yeah, it won't be the first time that forty-four whistle blow.
You know it sound just like, Baby, ain't gonner tell the truth no more.

J: *Tell me why you playing them blues like that.*
Say, I got a cabin, you know my room is number forty-four.
Love, I got a cabin, my room is number forty-four
Now when I wake up every morning, Baby, I declare the wolves steady knocking on my door.[9]

###

P: *This piano, she sticking on me, but I'm gonner try this country shack.*
I'm setting here a thousand miles from nowhere, in this one-room country shack.
I'm setting here a thousand miles from nowhere, in this one-room country shack.
J: *I'm here with you.*

Ain't nothing for my company but that old raggledy 'leven-foot wall.
I wake up every night about midnight, Love, I just can't sleep.
I wake up every night about midnight, Love, I just can't sleep.
All the crickets keep me company, you know the wind howling round my feet.
J: *Don't worry, Pine. Our day is coming.*
P: *I'm gonner play the blues.*
J: *Play the blues.*

I'm gonner git up early in the morning, I believe I'll git outta my bed.
I'm gonner git up early in the morning, I believe I'll git outta my bed.

I'm gonner find me a Clarksdale woman, if she blind and crippled and lame.
That's it, People![10]

#

J: *How you feeling this morning, Pine?*
P: *I'm feeling kind of down and out, man.*
J: *I know how it is. I hope we can git lucky, Pine.*
P: *Yeah. We gonner git lucky. My baby woke me up early this morning, and you know what she told me?*
J: *What'd she tell you?*
P: *She told me she wanted to rock one time.*
J: *Well, all right.*

Rock me, Baby, rock me all night long.
Rock me, Baby, rock me all night long.
I want you to rock me like my back don't have no bone.

Roll me, Baby, roll your wagon wheel.
Roll me, Baby, roll your wagon wheel.
I want you to roll me, Love, you don't know how it make me feel.

P: *Well, Love, I'm down in Mississippi and I got to play the blues.*
J: *I know what you mean, Pine. But soon as we git lucky, we'll cut out from here.*
P: *I'm telling you the truth, boy. I ain't gonner plow.*
I ain't gonner plow no mule no more.
J: *What you think about going out in California?*
P: *Yeah.*
J: *We gonner git lucky. Play the blues for me now.*

Rock me, Baby, rock your baby child.
Rock me, Baby, like I'm your baby child.
I want you to rock me like my back don't have no bone.

Looka here, Love.
See me coming, Baby, go git your rocking chair.

See me coming, Baby, go git your rocking chair.
You know I ain't no stranger 'cause I been living round with you.
Play it one more time.
J: *Play it good, Pine.*
P: *Well, all right.*[11]

⧣⧣⧣

J: *What's on your mind this morning, Pine?*
P: *Boy, I'm telling you, I'm thinking about the hard work.*
J: *Hard work?*
P: *Yeah.*

Love, I'm setting here a thousand miles from nowhere in this one-room country shack.
Yeah, now I'm setting here a thousand miles from nowhere in this one-room country shack.
J: *Why you so lonesome, Pine?*
P: *I got the blues.*
J: *How come?*
P: *My woman done quit me.*
You know the only thing I can confess, that old 'leven-foot raggledy cotton sack.

You know I wake up every night about midnight, Love, I just can't sleep.
I wake up every night about midnight, you know I just can't sleep.
You know all the crickets and frogs keep me company, you know the wind howling round my bed.

⧣⧣⧣

P: *I'm out on Mr. Jamison's place.*
J: *Driving that tractor for three dollars a day?*
P: *That's right. I'm gonner play the blues now, boy.*
J: *While you playing the blues, I want to ask you a question.*
You talk about Mr. Jamison. That's a big man. You mean he don't pay but three dollars a day?
P: *Two and a half.*
J: *For his best tractor driver?*

P: *The best one.*

J: *But when you was plowing that mule, you was doing that for nothing?*

P: *Dollar and a quarter.*

J: *That's the reason why you playing them blues today?*

P: *Yeah. I left there walking.*

J: *Where you trying to make your way to?*

P: *I'm trying to go to California.*

I'm gonner git up early in the morning, I believe I'll git outta my bed.

I'm gonner git up early in the morning, I believe I'll git outta my bed.

I'm gonner find me a Clarksdale woman, if she dumb and crippled and blind.

J: *Play the blues now and bring me a bottle of snuff.*

P: *One more time and I gotta go.*

⌗⌗⌗

P: *I'm gonner leave here, boy.*

J: *Yeah, let's go down to Vicksburg. I was down a little bit below here, coming toward Louisiana, and I looked up the road and I see a stick I thought was across the road, but it was a black snake.*

P: *Black snake?*

J: *Yeah, and I run up there and I went to kill the snake, and you know what the snake did? He throwed up both hands and told me don't hurt him 'cause he was trying to git outta Mississippi too.*[12]

P: *(laughs) I hear you.*

I got the blues for Vicksburg, Baby, sing 'em everywhere I go.

Now I got the blues for Vicksburg, sing 'em everywhere I go.

Now the reason I sing them blues, you know my woman don't love me no more.

I say Vicksburg's on a high hill, Louisiana just below,

I say Vicksburg's on a high hill, Louisiana just below.

P: *What you say, Love?*
J: *I hope we can make some money Saturday night.*
P: *Look here, Love.*
J: *Tell me about it.*

I say if you don't love me, Little Woman, why don't you tell me so?
You know I got more women, Baby, than a freight train can haul.

P: *Love, I'm gonner play the blues 'cause I'm moving on.*
J: *Tell me how they did you down in Vicksburg.*
P: *I'm going away.*
I say there ain't nothing I can do, ain't no more I can say.
There ain't nothing I can do, ain't nothing I can say.
I do all I can, Baby, you know, just to git along with you.
Good bye, Baby.[13]

♯♯♯

J: *Speaking of Vicksburg, Pine. I want to tell you something.*
P: *Yeah.*
J: *I remember when my grandmother was sold down in Decatur, Alabama. You know what happened?*
P: *What, boy?*
J: *They say they used to have old hymns. They would sing "There's no danger in the water." They was trying to git away then. Talking about that old hymn, Pine, "There's no danger in the water," well, you know what they meant then?*
P: *What did they mean?*
J: *They meant that Old Boss waddn't nowhere around. It would be one guy done got way over there. They'd be done set it up over night. "Well, we gonner leave here."*

They was making up a plot to git away, you know. You would hear one of them way over there, one of those guys would say, "Well, I know the Lord gonner help me."
P: *Yeah.*
J: *It meant that the other man that they was going to, he gonner meet them on the other side. You know what I mean? My grandmother, she was actually sold in that time and she brought my*

*daddy here from down in Decatur. Those old people, they would
sit overnight and they would talk and as they talked, they would
have one to git away and sing a verse. Right now I might tell
you, "Well, let's us go to Chicago."*

Well, we'd all say, "Okay. We're going to Chicago."

*But in those days the way they contacted each other was
through the hymns. They would be tired of this man. This man
done taken all of their earnings and they couldn't do anything
about it. My old grandmother, she used to sew quilts and set
down and she would tell me about it. That's really honest, you
know. She would say they had those songs when they wanted to
git over to each other. You know what I mean. They would start
the hymns. "Well, if the Lord don't help" or something like that.
They would be giving that word to another guy way over here.
They was pitching that sound backwards and forwards to one another so they could git away. You would hear one guy saying,
"Well, I'm gonner steal away."*[14]

⧣⧣⧣

J: *What you want do for me now?*
P: *I wanta dust my broom.*
J: *By meaning you gonner "dust that broom," is you gonner cut
out or you gonner stick around, Pine?*
P: *I'm gonner put my old lady to sweeping.*
J: *What's gonner happen to you?*

I'm gonner git up in the morning, believe I'll dust my broom.
I'm gonner git up in the morning, I believe I'll dust my broom.
My best woman quit me and my friends can have my room.

I'm gonner write a letter, telephone every town I know.
I'm gonner write a letter, telephone every town I know.
I gotta find my woman, she be in Ethiopia, I know.

J: *Why you gonner dust your broom?*
P: *My woman left me.*
J: *Why did she leave you?*
P: *I didn't treat her right.*

J: *Why don't you just tell it like it is. You didn't have the money to give her. You couldn't afford the money.*

I don't want no woman want every downtown man she meets.
I don't want no woman want every downtown man she meets.
She's a no-good doney, they shouldn't allow her on the street.

J: *Well, I ain't worried about one thing. If I git in trouble, I know my boss gonner git me out.*

I'm gonner go home. I believe, I believe my time ain't long.
I believe, I believe my time ain't long.
I believe, I believe my time ain't long.
I gotta call Mr. Harris, tell him please send my sow back home.[15]

⌗⌗⌗

J: *What about my boss, J. P. Davis? He's a good man.*
P: *What you say, man?*
J: *Mr. Harris is a good man.*
P: *But he don't put out no money.*
J: *Well, Davis ain't putting out none neither.*
P: *He'll loan you some, though.*
J: *Say, Pine, what happened in your child days?*
P: *Well, boy. I was plowing a mule and cutting stalks with a kaiser blade. Fifty cents a day. My daddy told me, "Son you can't feed yourself."*

I say, "Okay, Poppa. One day I'll be a man." I left. Left the mule in the field and told him goodbye.
J: *Told the mule goodbye?*
P: *"Goodbye. Goodbye. I don't never want to see you no more."*

But that mule got his pension before I got mine. He on welfare and I ain't.
J: *You still fooling with the mule?*
P: *No. I'm through with the mule.*
J: *In other words, you wouldn't tell the mule to "Git up" if he was setting in your lap.*
P: *If he was setting on my neck.*
J: *What would you tell him "Move"?*
P: *"Set on down."*

J: *Well, if he was running off with the world, what would you tell him?*

P: *"Save my part. I'll be there to reckly."*

⌗⌗⌗

[Pine Top begins playing the tune of "After Hours."]

J: *On this here right now, this "After Hours." We got a curfew. I want you to talk to me and play it and tell me about it. Other words, since the last time I seen you, I have moved up, and I come back to find out what was happening. I been to California and I'm doing pretty good. They tell me you "after hours" or something down here.*

P: *Yeah. I'm running late. They don't 'low me to stay up in Clarksdale after twelve o'clock. I'm gonner give the police a little bit of this "After Hours," you know, by Erskine Hawkins.*

J: *You mean that's why you playing that, because they don't 'low you to stay up after hours. Look here, man. It ain't but ten o'clock now. What time you have to go to bed?*

P: *I have to go to bed at twelve o'clock.*

J: *You mean you got to go to bed and you can't be up?*

P: *I got to go.*

F: *Wait a minute, man. Let's correct that. This town is open now.*

P: *I know it is now. But it didn't used to be.*

J: *You say this town's open now?*

F: *Yes sir. All night long.*

J: *But where you going, though? You can't find a drink.*

P: *Boy, you better hush talking so loud. Mr. Billy's gonner hear you. It's eleven o'clock. I'm going to Nashville, where I can git with the wee wee hours. Let me play it one time.*

J: *Pine, you got a chance to go head on out to California with me if you want to.*

P: *I'm going. Put the light out.*

J: *You playing the blues. Pine, but you ain't telling me nothing about it.*

P: *I'm fixing to go now.*

J: *You mess with my woman, I'll make my butcher knife eat you up.*

⌗⌗⌗

F: *Whip out some sound, Pine.*
J: *Is I got a soul brother in the house?*
F: *Aw yeah, man. Aw yeah.*

Big Boss, don't you hear me when I call?
Big Boss, don't you hear me when I call?
Yes, you ain't all that tall, you just big, that's all.

You long-legged, you just make a fuss.
You just fucking round, trying to be someone.
Big Boss Man, don't you hear me when I call?
Yes you long and tall, you ain't gitting nowhere.
J: *Saturday night!*

Now you try to take my woman, you ain't doing no good.
Running round here talking, trying to be someone.
Now, Big Boss Man, don't you hear me when I call?
Now you ain't that strong, you just big, that's all.[16]

P: *I'm going, Love.* [Continues playing tune.]
J: *Just before you go, I wanta tell you something.*
P: *What you wanta tell me, Love?*
J: *There was a real good-looking guy that had plenty of money
and good-looking women. So a strange lady came in and she
asked this other lady why this good-looking man ain't married.
She say, "Well, he ain't found nobody here he want to marry."
"Aw yeah? Y'all ain't treating him right."
So this lady, she walked up to him and asked, "Why you ain't
married?"
He said, "Well, I'm looking for a lady got two of them things."
"Aw yeah? Me and you gonner git married."
He told her, "Well, come on to the house Friday night when I
git paid off."*
P: *She come over there that Friday night.*
F: *What'd she tell him?*
J: *She said, "Well here I is."
He said, "Is you got two of 'em?"*

She told him, "Yeah, I got two."
"All right. Pull off your clothes and git in the bed."
So she hit the bed. She gived him that on the top first, and when he got through, she turned over and turned her back on him and told him, "Git this one."
He got that one too. That was on a Friday night. The same thing happened on Saturday and Sunday night. That Monday morning she told him, "Baby, before you go to work, let's booze some."
He said, "All right, baby."
So she gone downtown and bought some booze. She got off from the house a little piece and she looked at her money and said, "Well, what you told me to git? I ain't got enough money. What you want me to do, sell one of them things?"
He said, "Yeah, baby. That's all right."
She walked off a little piece further and he stopped her. He called and said, "Hey. Wait a minute, honey. I'll tell you what you do. You sell both of them sons-of-bitches 'cause I'm through with them."
Go 'head and play, Pine!
P: *Big Boss Man!*

⸨⸨⸨

P: *I'm gonner play me a boogie. I ain't played no boogie.*
F: *Work out some sound.*

Now do what I tell you.
You talking about that Pine Top Boogie Woogie
I'm gonner tell you all about it.
I say stop, I mean stop.
I say git it, I mean git it.
You know what I'm talking about.
Now look. See that woman with the red dress on?
F: *Yeah, man.*
I want you to swing her right on back to me.
F: *Come here, baby.*
Don't forgit it, Son.
F: *Yeah.*
I say hold it. I mean hold it.

F: *I got it.*
I say stop. I mean everybody do the stop.
Now, Red, hold yourself. Don't move a peg.
Git it.
Now boogie.

Everybody running around here talking about that Pine Top Boogie Woogie.
I'm gonner tell you about it.
Cause I was over with Mr. Harris and I hit that mule.
I learned how to hit it, and then I learned how to play that Pine Top Boogie Woogie.
J: *Yeah. Boogie woogie all night long.*
Now look, there is something in this town I want everybody to know.
This is Mr. Roosevelt Sykes what's playing.
I say hold it, I mean stop.
Now, Love, hold yourself.
Don't move a peg, Love.
Now, Floyd, you can have it.

I'm tell you one thing, I'm gonner play this Pine Top Boogie Woogie.
I'm fixing to leave Clarksdale. I'm going to California.
I may go out in Texas.
Now, Love, hold it one more time.
Don't move a peg.
Now go head and boogie.[17]

❋❋❋

J: *I been gone away from here two years and now I own a Cadillac. Play the old road blues now.*
P: *Shore nuff?*
J: *Yes sir. Find that snuff-dipping key.*
P: *Let's leave on that Santa Fe.*

I say Mobile on that Southern Line, Jackson on that Santa Fe.
I say Mobile on that Southern Line, Jackson on that Santa Fe.

You know I got a woman in Tutwiler, I got a woman in Sumner too.
I say Lord have mercy, please git me way from here.
I say Lord have mercy, please git me way from here.
I done got tired of working on Mr. Harris, working for five dollars a day.
P: *Talk to me now.*

Early in the morning, that Santa Fe gonner run.
I say early in the morning, you know that Santa Fe gonner run.
If I don't carry my woman, Love, you know I'm gonner carry my little Juicy Fruit.

I say the engineer blowed the whistle, you know the fireman, he rung too.
That must of been my baby, Love, she was gitting off that old Seventy-Two.

My baby got a thirty-eight, and she got a thirty-two-twenty too.
My baby got a thirty-eight, and she got a thirty-two-twenty too.
Say if she put me in the graveyard, I declare she won't have to go to jail.

I say early in the morning, they tell me that Santa Fe shore gonner run.
I say early in the morning, that Santa Fe shore gonner run.
I say it took my woman, come back and got my used-to-be.
J: *You make me think of when I used to walk through ice and snow. But I done got lucky. I don't have to do it no more.*
P: *What say, Love?*
J: *I know what make you play 'em like that.*
P: *I got the blues.*
J: *Man drive up to your door soon in the morning telling you to go to work. Then he come all up in the house, sitting there where you and your wife at.*
P: *I'm telling you.*
J: *That was Ole Boss.*
P: *I'm gonner tell about that.*

You know my woman done got funny, she don't want me to have
my pussy.
My woman done got funny, Love, she don't want me to have my
pussy.
She cook cornbread for her husband, she cook biscuits for her
man.

You should of been down here in nineteen and thirty-five.
You should of been down here in nineteen and thirty-five.
J: *What happened?*
The womens was quitting the mens and didn't have no place to
hide.
Merry Christmas, see what Santa Claus gonner bring.
I say Merry Christmas, see what Santa Claus gonner bring.
He may bring you a apple, Baby, and he might not bring you a
doggone thing.

P: *Tell her to come back, Love.*
J: *You been disappointed a many Christmas by Santa Claus,
haven't you?*
P: *My stocking had ashes in it.*
J: *Come on and go with me and you can git it filled up.*[18]
P: *Where we going?*
J: *We going where they open the door and let all them Chris-
tians out.*
P: *What?*
J: *With them angels. I don't do nothing now but ride a Cadillac.
I'm a Mississippi boy, but I done skipped from it now.*

Well I got my ticket, and my suitcase all ready to go.
You know I got my ticket, and my suitcase all ready to go.
I'm gonner catch my baby, we gonner ride that Santa Fe.
All right, Love.

J: *You remember what happened in 'thirty-five, Pine? That's
when the panic was on. You couldn't git a can of Prince Albert
tobacco. Fifty cents a day on the levee. The women was leaving
the mens and couldn't git nowhere. No bus running.*
F: *That must of been in President Hoover's time?*

P: *It was in Hoover's time.*
J: *That was the time of that N.R.A. or something like that.*
P: *Oh, it waddn't then. Roosevelt put that on. Hoover took all the money and wouldn't feed nothing but a mule and a hog.*
J: *And they belonged to him?*
P: *Yeah. Womens couldn't wear dresses. They had to wear cotton sacks, them sacks they used to pick cotton in.*
J: *You mean that rough material?*
P: *Cotton sacks. That's right.*

###

You used to be sweetest girl I ever known.
Looked to me, you want to be left on your own.
Now you gone away and left me, you make me go through black night.

Used to be, I could call you on the phone.
Me and you, our work was almost done.
Now you gone away and left me, you wanta be on your own, black night.
Play the blues, Love.

J: *I'm shore glad we up here on Seventy-ninth and Cottage Grove where we can be free. I believe I'll take you to WVON. That's down on Cicero in Chicago, Illinois.*

Used to be, I could call you my own.
Looked to me, your love is almost gone.
Now you gone away and left me, you wanta be by yourself, black night.

J: *Boy, you playing that just like my brother, Willie. Why you play "Black Night" like that, Pine?*
P: *Done got late now. We going with the blues.*

Used to be, I could call you mine alone.
Looked to me, you was my all alone.
Now you a mess, Baby, you make me go through black night.[19]

COMPOSERS

Scott Dunbar, Lake Mary.

Tom Dumas, Tutwiler.

"Little Son" Jefferson, Leland.

James "Black Boy" Hughes, Centreville.

Joe "Big Daddy" Louis, WOKJ, Jackson.

J. W. "Sonny Boy" Watson, Leland.

B. B. King at Lucifer's, Boston.

CLARKSDALE BLUES

Jasper Love home.

Jook joint.

Willie and Jasper Love (l. to r.).

Downtown Clarksdale.

Family photographs.

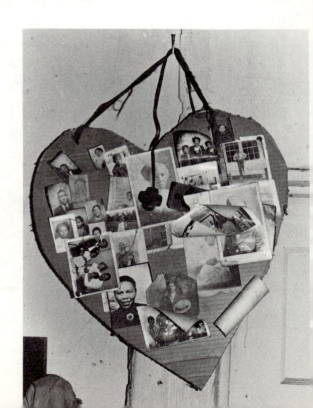

⋕⋕⋕

Love, I've had my fun if I don't git well no more.
J: *Long as you stay in Mississippi, you never will git well.*
I have had my fun if I don't git well no more.
You know my head is killing me and I'm going down slow.

I want you to write my mother, tell her the shape I'm in.
Want you to write my mother, tell her the shape I'm in.
Tell her to pray for me, Love, forgive me for all my sins.
J: *Man, you must be broke and hungry, raggledy and dirty too.*
P: *I'm in bad shape.*

Tell her don't send me no doctor, doctor can't do no good.
Tell her don't send me no doctor, doctor can't do no good.
You know it's all my fault, I didn't do the things that I should.

J: *What about this Old Granddaddy Eighty-six [whiskey]? Will
that help you any?*
P: *Yeah, boy. I know one thing. I may not git well, but I am
gonner try to git well.*
J: *You can have a good feeling.*
P: *I'm trying to tell you.*

Now on the next train south, Love, look for my clothes back
home.
J: *You don't wanta go south.*
On the next train south, look for my clothes back home.
If you don't see my body, Floyd, you can view my bones.

J: *Tell him to go west or north, but don't go south.*
Now, Mother, don't you worry, this is all over now.
Mother, don't you worry, this is all over now.
You know your son is lost out in this world somewhere.

P: *That's all, Love.*
J: *Play it and talk to me a little bit. Man, you must be worried
to play the blues like that.*
P: *I'm is, boy. You know one thing?*

J: *What?*
P: *The doctor said I waddn't gonner live long. So I'm trying to tell you.*

On the next train south, look for my clothes back home.
On the next train south, look for my clothes back home.
If you don't see my body, you can view my bones.
Good bye![20]

♯♯♯

Well I don't want a lot. I just want a little bit.
J: *Little bit of what?*
Well I don't want a lot. I just want a little bit.
I just want a little bit, just a teenie weenie bit, teenie weenie bit of your love.
Turn your lamp down low, it's gitting late at night.
I love you, Baby, don't you hear my prayers?
Just a teenie weenie bit, teenie weenie bit of your love.

F: *Work out.*
J: *Go head, soul brother.*

I love you, Baby, and I'm sick at night.
I love you, Baby, and I'm sick at night.
Just a teenie weenie bit, teenie weenie bit of your love.

Well I don't want it all, just want a teenie weenie bit.
I don't want it all, just want a little bit.
Just a teenie weenie bit, teenie weenie bit of your love.[21]

♯♯♯

P: *Say, Floyd.*
F: *Yeah, man.*
P: *You know one thing, boy?*
F: *What's that?*
P: *I'm drifting.*
F: *You must be going somewhere.*

J: *He's trying to drift outta Mississippi. I know what he's trying to do.*

You know I'm drifting and I'm drifting just like a ship out on the sea.

Well I'm drifting and I'm drifting like a ship out on the sea.

Well you know I ain't got nobody in this world to care for me.

J: *Tell me, Pine.*

If my baby only take me back again. (She done quit me, Floyd.)

If my baby only take me back again.

Well she say I ain't good, I haven't got no friend.

J: *You mean you working all day, but ain't making no money?*

I give her all my money, tell me what more can I do?

I give her all my money, tell me what more can I do?

Now you a good woman, Baby, but you just won't be true.

J: *You can't do no more, man. You can't do no more.*

I say bye, bye, Baby. Baby, bye, bye, bye.

Bye, bye, Baby. Tell you bye, bye, bye.

Now it gonner be too late and I'll be so far away.[22]

J: *Play it. I don't care what happens. Play the blues all night long.*

P: *Bye, Baby.*

♯♯♯

P: *I'm gonner try this old blues now.*

Let me tell you, Baby, tell what I will do.

Rob, steal and kill somebody just to git home to you.

Ain't that loving you, Baby?

Ain't that loving you, Baby?

Ain't that loving you, Baby, and you don't even know my name.

They may kill me, Baby, do me like they used to do.

My body might rise and swim to the ocean and come back home to you.

Ain't that loving you, Baby?

Ain't that loving you, Baby?
Ain't that loving you, Baby, and you don't even know my
name.[23]

J: *Aw yeah. That's loving all right.*
F: *Work out, Pine.*
J: *Love her in your own way.*
P: *I'm gonner play it one more time.*

♯♯♯

J: *Have a Saturday night ball.*
P: *What's that, Love?*
J: *Sunday night you gotta go to sleep 'cause you gotta git up
and go to work Monday morning.*
You know the war is over, I'm going down that sunny road.
J: *Done got tired of soldiering now.*
F: *Wait a minute, man. They still fighting in Vietnam.*
I say the war is over, I'm going down that sunny road.
I done got tired of Clarksdale, working for my room and board.
J: *I know what you mean, man.*

I say when I was making good money, you treat me like I was a
king.
J: *She lied to you then.*
When I was making good money, Darling, you treat me like I
was a king.
J: *Then what happened?*
Now you know all my money gone, and your love don't mean a
thing.

Hey, Baby, bring me my hat and coat.
I can feel the green grass growing under your doorstep.
You know this time tomorrow I'll be way down that sunny road.

Well I done did all, I did all I could afford.
You know I done did all, I did all I could afford.
You know this time tomorrow, Baby, I'll be down that sunny
road.

J: *Work that bass again for me, Pine.*
P: *What you say, Love?*
J: *I hear you now. I see you buying a ticket, man. Where you fixing to go?*
P: *I'm going to Chicago.*
J: *The West Side or the South Side?*
P: *I'm going to the South.*

Bye, bye, Baby, I did all I could for you.
Bye, bye, Baby, I did all I could for you.
You's a bad-headed woman and I don't want you no more.[24]

J: *If you going to the South Side, you must be going over to Stoney Island where it's happening at.*
P: *Yeah, boy. I got my ticket.*
F: *Man, you better go on the North Side. They raising hell on the South Side.*
J: *Detroit is on fire and Chicago is burning down.*

⌗⌗⌗

P: *Let me see what I wanta do.*
J: *What's fixing to happen, Pine?*
P: *How 'bout "Juicy Fruit"?*
J: *Go 'head. You's a free man. You ain't got nothing to worry about.*
F: *Your way or the highway.*
P: *Here I go.*
J: *Work that bass way down.*
Hello, Juicy Fruit, how do you do?
Hello, Juicy Fruit, how do you do?
You remember me? I remember you.

Hello, Juicy Fruit, how do you do?
Hello, Juicy Fruit, how do you do?
Do you remember me? I remember you.
I used to carry you by here, by the railroad too.[25]

⌗⌗⌗

I wants to know how much longer, Baby, have I got to wait on
you.
I wants to know how much longer, Baby, have I got to wait on
you.
How long, how long, how much more long?

I lay down last night, I saw you in my sleep.
I lay down last night, I saw you in my sleep.
I began to wondering what do you want with me.

How long, how much more long?
How long, how much more long?
How long, now, you want your rolling done?
J: *If you should die before your time what would happen?*
P: *What you say, Love?*
J: *If you die before your time, remember she'd be ever on your
mind.*

If I should die, die before my time,
J: *Well, all right.*
If I should die, die before my time,
I want you to know what will become of me.

I lay down last night, I missed you in my arms.
I lay down last night, I missed you in my arms.
I began to wonder what do you think of me.
J: *Push way back and gimme some of that low bass now.*

How long, how much more long, how long?
How long, how much more long, how long?
How long, how long you want your loving done?

I wants to know how much more longer, Baby, have I got to
wait on you.
I wants to know how much more longer, Baby, have I got to
wait on you.
How long, now, Baby, you want your loving done?[26]
P: *What you say, Floyd?*
F: *I hear you, Pine. Work out.*

P: *How long!*
J: *Don't stop now. Gimme one of them good road blues.*
P: *Good road blues coming up. I wants to know why my baby
always play around.*

I wonder, Baby, why don't you settle down.
I wants to know.
I wants to know.
I just got to know.

Look like you got me flunking, if I'm wrong, please tell me so.
I know I was wrong, but some day I will realize.
I wants to know.
I wants to know.
I just got to know.

I used to believe what you'd tell me.
I used to believe every word you say.
But look like from your way, I believe you gonner put me down.
I wants to know.
I wants to know.
I just got to know.
Now I wants to know, Floyd.[27]

⧉⧉⧉

P: *Remember that, Love? Remember that, Buddy? Let me git
another good blues now. I'm gonner play the blues one more
time.*
J: *Let me hear you, Pine Top.*
F: *Work out. Work out, Pine. Let your hair down now.*

Yes, my baby love to boogie, I love to boogie too.
Say, my baby love to boogie, I love to boogie too.
I'm gonner boogie this time and I ain't gonner boogie no more.
J: *Well, all right.*

You know she do that boogie and shout it down through the
street.
She doos that boogie and shout it down through the street.

She howls so loud they run up and down the street.
Boogie one time.

Don't the sun look lonesome, shining down through the tree.
Don't the sun look lonesome, shining down through the tree.
Don't your hair look lovely when you put it back up for me.
[Maudie Shirley and Baby Sister enter the room.]
J: *Well, all right. Look who just come in. Work out, Pine.*
F: *Look like we got to shore nuff boogie now.*
I love my baby and I tell the world I do.
M: *Do you really, Darling?*
I love my baby and I tell the world I do.
M: *I wanta marry you.*
Well I hope she'll come to love me too.
M: *I already do.*

♯♯♯

Next time I see you, things won't be the same.
Next time I see you, things won't be the same.
If it hurts you, Darling, you only have yourself to blame.

(Maudie)
You know you lied, cheated, oh so long.
You know you lied, cheated, oh so long.
You just a no-good man, you only have yourself to blame.

(Maudie)
Next time you see me, things won't be the same.
Next time you see me, things won't be the same.
If it hurts you, Darling, you only have yourself to blame.

(Maudie and Pine Top)
Well you lied, you cheated, oh so long.
Well you lied, you cheated, oh for so long.
You just no-good, you only have yourself to blame.
M: *Work out, baby.*

You drink your whiskey, I'll drink my wine.
You tend to your business, Baby, I'll tend to mine.
Next time you see me, things won't be the same.

J: *What you got against the girl?*
P: *She's a heartbreaker.*

(Maudie)
Yes, next time you see me, things won't be the same.
If it hurt you . . . My Darling, you only have yourself to
blame.[28]

⌗⌗⌗

I say God made a elephant, he made him big and stout.
Waddn't satisfied till he made his snout.
He made his snout, made it long and round.
Waddn't satisfied till he made his tail.
He made his tail, made it to fan the fly.
Waddn't satisfied till he made his eye.
He made his eye, made it to look on the grass.
Waddn't satisfied till he made his ass.
He made his ass so he could stick in his dick.
Waddn't satisfied till he made his prick.
He made his prick, made it hard as a rock.
His nuts would crack when he coughed a lot.
He's a dirty little man.
He's a dirty little man.
Dirty little man.[29]

Children round the house having a fit.
Your mother in the house making jam outta shit.
She's a nasty little woman.
She's a nasty little woman.
Dirty little woman as you'll find.

I want all you women, want you to fall in line.
I want you to shake it like I shake mine.
Shake it quick, Baby, shake it fast.
If you can't shake it quick, shake your little black ass.
You a dirty little woman.
Dirty little woman to me.

I had your momma, your sister too.
I throwed a brick at your old man too.

He's a running old man.
He's a running old man.
He's a running old man, running old man.

I want all you women, want you to fall in line.
I want you to shake like I shake mine.
Shake it quick, Baby, shake it fast.
If you can't shake it quick, shake your little black ass.
Shake your little ass.
You a shaking little woman, shaking little woman.

Sitting round the house and tote that brick.
Your momma in the kitchen making jam outta shit.
She's a nasty little woman.
She's a nasty little woman.
She's a nasty little woman, nasty little woman to me.

P: *I'm fixing to put "Running Wild" on there.*
M: *Aw, Baby. I got words for you. You gonner run wild?*
P: *Running wild.*
M: *I know you ain't gonner run wild all your life. I'll slow you down one of these days.*

Listen here, Woman, where'd you stay last night?
It ain't none of your business.
You know you ain't treating me right.
Aw, Woman, Baby, you steady running wild.
Now the baby I'm loving, she don't treat me right.

M: *You got the nerve to tell me I'm running wild?*
P: *What you say?*

(Maudie)
When I stay at home every day, trying to treat you right,
You come home late at night, jump on me and there's a fight.
Baby, you know, you know that ain't right.

P: *What say, Baby?*
M: *You heard me.*

Say, I work hard every day, bring home my pay.
You tell me, Baby, I got nowhere to stay.
Now looka here, Baby, you know you running wild.
You just running round, Baby, Baby, you ain't no good.

M: *Yeah, Baby. I know just what you mean. You must think I'm
a fool, don't you?*
P: *Naw. I don't.*
M: *Yeah, I know you think I'm a fool.*
P: *I love you, Baby.*
M: *I don't love you, Darling.*
P: *Why, Baby?*
M: *'Cause you always doing me wrong.*
P: *Ha ha!*

Now tell me, Woman, what you got on your mind.
Tell me, Woman, what you got on your mind.
M: *Nothing but loving, Baby.*
The way you treat me, you just running wild.
J: *Better see me then.*

(Maudie)
Well I'll tell you this one thing, Baby.
If you love me, Darling, I'll do anything you say.
If you love me, Darling, I'll do anything you say.
But as long as you messing up, Baby, I don't have no say.

I'm gonner tell you now, Baby, ain't gonner tell you no more.
I'm gonner tell you now, Baby, ain't gonner tell you no more.
Well you running wild, Baby, you just got to go.

P: *What you say about that, Baby?*
M: *Well you got your womens, why can't I have my mens?*
P: *I don't like that.*
M: *Neither do I.*
P: *You oughta not do that. I'm gonner finish up.*
J: *That's just like a woman.*
M: *Let me tell you one thing.*
P: *What you say, Honey?*

M: *Baby, you know I love you.*
P: *I love you too, Honey.*
M: *Don't worry, Darling. We'll make it.*
P: *Goodbye, Baby.*
M: *See you later, Sugar.*

♯♯♯

Rock me, Baby, rock me all night long.
Rock me, Baby, rock me all night long.
I want you to rock me like my back don't have no bone.

Roll me, Baby, roll your wagon wheel.
Roll me, Baby, roll your wagon wheel.
I want you to roll me, you don't know how it makes me feel.
Play it, Baby Sister.
J: *Work out, Pine.*

See me coming, better git your rocking chair.
See me coming, better git your rocking chair.
Baby, you know I ain't no stranger 'cause I'm used to living here.
Play it, Baby Sister.

F: *Go head on, Pine.*

Rock me, Baby, rock me all night long.
Rock me, Baby, rock me all night long.
I want you to rock me like my back ain't got no bone.
Roll me, Baby, roll your wagon wheel.
Roll me, Baby, roll your wagon wheel.
I want you to roll me, you don't know how it make me feel.
Play it, Baby Sister, one time.
Aw, rock me, Baby.[30]

♯♯♯

(Maudie)
Yeah, See, See See Rider
Yeah, see what you done done.
Yeah, yeah, yeah, See, See See Rider,
See what you have done.

Well you made me love you,
Now your man has come.

Yes, I'm going away, Baby, and I won't be back till fall.
Yeah, yeah, yeah, going away, Baby, and I won't be back till fall.
If I find me a good boy, I won't be back at all.

Yeah, See, See See Rider,
Yeah, see what you have done.
Yeah, yeah, yeah, See See Rider.
See what you have done.[31]

⚏⚏⚏

P: *All right now. We going with some Louis Jordan.*
M: *"Ain't That Just Like a Woman." I know what it is. I know*
everything he sing.

There was Eve and Adam happy as can be.
Eve got up under that apple tree.
Ain't that just like a woman.
Ain't that just like a woman.
Ain't that just like a woman, they'll do it every time.
F: *Do what, Pine?*

You been gitting money on the side.
With all I give you, you ain't satisfied.
Ain't that just like a woman.
Ain't that just like a woman.
Ain't that just like a woman, they'll do it every time.
Now play a little bit!

All them young ones with their mammy at the gate.
They was down there crying for bread.
Said Elijah come to the door and said let them children git something to eat.

Ain't that just like a woman.
Ain't that just like a woman.
Ain't that just like a woman, they'll do it every time.

That's just like a woman.
F: *Do it every time.*

⌗⌗⌗

P: *Well, I'm going.*
Let me tell you, tell you what I will do.
Rob, steal, and kill somebody just to git back home to you.
Ain't that loving you, Baby?
Ain't that loving you, Baby?
Ain't that loving you, Baby, and you don't even know my name.

They may kill me, Baby, Baby, like they used to do.
My body might rise and swim to the ocean and come on home to
you.
Now ain't that loving you, Baby?
Ain't that loving you, Baby?
Ain't that loving you and you don't even know my name.

(Maudie)
Let me tell you, Baby, what I'm gonner do.
Swim the ocean, Baby, to git back home to you.
Ain't that loving you, Baby?
Ain't that loving you, Baby?
Ain't that loving you, Baby, and you don't even know my name.

P: *Play the blues.*
F: *Play it, Pine.*

Let me tell you, Baby, tell you what I will do.
Rob, steal, and kill somebody just to git home to you.
Now ain't that loving you, Baby?
Ain't that loving you, Baby?
Ain't that loving you, Baby, and you don't even know my name.
That's all![32]

⌗⌗⌗

(Maudie)
Early one morning, the skies was blue.
Down through the alley the shitwagon flew.

Waddn't a sound heard.
Pine got hit by a flying turd.
Baby that's all right.
He told me that was all right.
Well we was down on Funky Broadway one day.
They was having a good dinner down there.
Do y'all know what they was having?
They was having some French fried potatoes,
Some inner-tube sausage,
Bow-wow spaghetti,
Blowed-out beans,
A sign off a chicken platter called a red-ball tube.
They put it in the loup,
and took it to the country,
and got the cow for two.
That's down on Funky Broadway.
Yeah, Baby, you going down there too?
They have a good dessert.
They having wind pie,
Shitty gum smothered down in do-do soup.
If you like that, Baby,
Go down on the four round corners.

Listen, I'm gonner tell you what the preacher told us yesterday.
He got up in church and said these words.
He said "Ladies and Gentlemules,
"I stand before you as I stand behind you,
"To tell you of something I know nothing about.
"Next Thursday is Good Friday.
"They having fathers' meeting for mothers only.
"If you can come, please stay at home.
"Wear your best, if you haven't any.
"Admission free, pay at the door.
"Come in, have a seat, set your damn ass on the floor.
"That's at four round corners, Baby."
Work out, Sugar [to Pine Top].[33]

(Pine Top)
Up she run and down she fell.

Her legs flew open like a mussel shell.
Cause she a dirty little woman.
She a dirty little woman.[34]

M: *Let me tell you this, man.*
P: *What?*
M: *Let me tell you what happened.*

(Maudie)
Momma kilt a chicken, she thought it was a duck.
Put that thing on the table with his leg sticking up.
You got to bottle up and go.
Yeah, you got to bottle up and go.
Cause when momma kilt that chicken she had to bottle up and
go.[35]

P: *Why was that?*
M: *She was full of booze.*

♯♯♯

Let me tell you, Ladies, what I must do.
Everybody tell me in your neighborhood,
That you got good business.
That you got good business.
You got good business, think I'm gonner trade with you.

If you do business and you can't do it right,
Don't ring around in your arms all night.
Cause you got good business.
Cause you got good business.
You got good business, I wants to trade with you.
J: *I hear you.*

Looka here, Baby, what you trying to do?
Make me love you and I don't want to.
Cause you got good business.
Cause you got good business.
You got good business, I wants to trade with you.

\# \# \#

P: *This is the old blues I'm coming with now. Y'all don't know
nothing about this.*

How long, Baby, how long,
Has that evening train been gone?
How long, how long?

I woke this morning, I sit and mourned.
Thought about the good times I have known.
How long, how long, how long?
F: *Work out, Pine.*

I can see the green grass growing up on the hill.
Ain't none of the green grass for a dollar bill.
How long, how long, Baby, how long?

I'm going up on the mountain, like a mountain jack.
I'm gonner call my baby back.
How long, how long, Baby, how long?

How long, Baby, how long,
Has that evening train been gone?
How long, how long?

Worked all the summer and all the fall
I had to take up my old guitar.
How long, how long?[36]

\# \# \#

Now the war is over, I'm going down that sunny road.
I say the war is over, I'm going down that sunny road.
You know I ain't making nothing in Clarksdale,
Baby, but my room and board.

Now when I was making good, you treat me like I was a king.
When I was making good, you treat me like I was a king.

Now you know I ain't got no war-plant job,
My love don't mean a thing.

P: *Play the blues. Maudie, we going to Louisiana, ain't we?*
F: *I'm going to git me a mojo hand.*

Now, Baby, I'm gone you can cry your blues away.
Baby, I'm gone, you can cry your blues away.
I'll find some other, Darling, gonner let you have your way.

Bring me my hat and coat.
M: *Don't forgit your shoes.*
I can feel the green grass growing under your doorstep.
You know this time tomorrow I'll be way down.

Well I done did all, I did all I could do.
M: *Don't tell that lie.*
Well I done did all, I did all I could do.
You know this time tomorrow, I'll be down where I want to.

BS: *He told me he'd give me fifty dollars.*
M: *I don't know how. He told you the same thing he told me.*
BS: *What you talking about?*
M: *That's a thing he got going on.*
BS: *Who you want, Pine, me or her?*
P: *I want you.*
BS: *All right then.*
M: *You mean to tell me you don't want me now?*
J: *Somebody ain't doing their bed work right here.*
M: *He's cutting me off with that damn music.*
J: *If Pine can't take care of y'all, come to my home.*
BS: *We don't wanta come to your home. We like Pine's home.*
J: *I do some mighty good things. I'll hold your legs up and ride you all night long.*

Bye bye, Baby, I did all I could afford.
M: *Oh, Darling, don't leave me.*
Bye bye, Baby, I did all I could afford.

M: *Darling, please don't leave me.*
You know this time tomorrow, I'll be down that sunny road.[37]

※※※

P: *Let's have some toasts. Who gonner say the first? You go.*

(Maudie)
It was early one morning when the sky was blue.
It was dark in Clarksdale when among the flying herd,
Bill got hit by a flying turd.
Up jumped the monkey from the cocoanut tree.
He had keen-toed shoes and a spinach coat.
He was a sharp-looking monkey and that waddn't no joke.

※※※

(Pine Top)
All the insects give a ball.
The chinch was the doorman.
The grasshopper was the floorwalker.
The Tommy Turd was the last man got there.
The Tommy Turd come and knocked on the door.
He say "Say, Mr. Chinch, can I come in?"
He say "No."
He say "Please let me come in.
Man, I'll come and set on the nail keg, and I won't move."

The bessie bug told Tommy Turd to see the grasshopper.
The grasshopper sided up to the door.
Tommy Turd said "Mr. Grasshopper, can I come in to that ball?"
"No, Big Boy. They tell me everywhere you go you just want
to show your ass."
He said "Please let me come in. I'll set on the nail keg and I
won't move."
The grasshopper told the Tommy Turd to come on in.
The bessie bug jumped down on the piano and commenced to
beating out the naptime boogie woogie.
Way after a while the Tommy Turd swung his foot and hit the
floor.

He say "Hey, Love, I want you to play me the ass-dragging blues cause I feel like rolling."

⌗⌗⌗

(Maudie)
There was two ladies setting out on the damn bank one day. They was fishing. One said to the other old lady, "It's time to go home."
"No, I'm gonner stay till a little later."
The other lady went on home. Her friend was sitting out there and you know how those old-timey ladies wore long dresses with no drawers. She had both feet cocked up on the bank fishing. It was two bullfrogs out in the middle of the lake. It was gitting late over in the evening. One bullfrog said to the other one, "Hey, man. It's getting pretty late. Let's find a hole to go in."
The other bullfrog say, "Hey, man."
"Hey, man, what?"
"I see two holes setting over there. You go in one and I go in other'n."
"Where 'bout, man?"
"Right up under that curtain over there."
So sure enough, one bullfrog jumped in her pussy and the other jumped in her asshole. The lady went home, and along about two o'clock that morning her husband decided he'd have intercourse with her.
J: *What is intercourse?*
M: *They fucked. Put it that way.*
J: *All right.*
'Bout four o'clock that morning the frogs decided they'd hop out back down to the lake. They hopped on back down to the lake. The big frog said to the little frog, "Hey, man."
"What's that?"
"How did you sleep last night?"
"Man, let me tell you something. I didn't sleep worth a damn."
"Me either."
"What happened to you?"
"Let me tell you something. Long about two o'clock a son-of-a-

bitch come in there and tried to root me out of there. I tried to get out, but it was two sacks over the damn hole and I couldn't get out and I had to stay there until this morning.

"Aw, man. You ain't been in no hell yet. Let me tell you something. Along about that same time that son-of-a-bitch tried to root you out, they tried to root me out too. I pushed and I shoved, and I pushed again and I shoved again trying to git out, and I hauled off and bit the motherfucker. And do you know what he did to me?"

"Naw, man. What?"

"That son-of-a-bitch hauled off and puked in my face."

⌗⌗⌗

(Floyd)
I waddn't invited, but I'm down here.
I ain't dressed so fine, but I'm around here.
I'm so happy, look like I could shout and shit.
And ain't a son-of-a-bitch in here can put me out.

⌗⌗⌗

I know a old lady, she lived on a hill.
Shitted in a stocking, and she carried it to the mill.
Told the old man to don't take no toll,
'Cause it may come a double-asshole.

⌗⌗⌗

(Maudie)
Let me tell all y'all something.
I hate to talk about your mammy.
A good old soul.
Got a grass pussy and a bull asshole.
I remember your momma didn't have no stove.
Cooked flapjacks on her pussy hole.
I remember your momma fucked a dick of bologna.
Had ninety-nine cows and one Shetland pony.[38]
J: Don't talk about my momma. My daddy loves her.

⌗⌗⌗

(Floyd)
I am a fucking pee eye.
I wear my fucking clothes.
Once I went uptown one day, the police caught me fucking.
I say, "Police, what is my fine?"
He said, "Ninety-nine dollars and one fucking dime."
I say, "Look, Police, you take this ninety-nine dollars and one
fucking dime,
"'Cause you may catch this poor child fucking most any time."
Go on!

⌗⌗⌗

J: *Play a blues.*

Baby, please don't go.
Baby, please don't go.
Baby, please don't go back to New Orleans.

You got me way down here.
You got me way down here.
You got me way down here, just treat me like a dog.
J: *Sing out, Pine.*

Turn your lamp down low.
Turn your lamp down low.
I beg you all night long, Baby please don't go.

Before I be your dog.
Before I be your dog.
Before I be your dog, I make you walk the log.
Baby, please don't go.
F: *Go head on, Pine.*[39]

⌗⌗⌗

I say the gypsy woman told my mammy, fore I was born,
"You got a boy-child coming, for a son-of-a-gun.
"He gonner make all young women call him by the name.
"The world gonner know what it's all about."
You know everbody knows I'm here.

I'm your hoochie-koochie man, Baby Sister, everybody knows I'm here.

J: *Work out, Pine.*

I got a black-cat bone.
Got a mojo too.
Got a John the Conquer Root.
I'm gonner mess with you.
I'm gonner make you women take me by the hand.
Everybody hollering I'm the hoochie-koochie man.
Yeah, everybody knows I'm the man.

I'm your hoochie-koochie man.
Everybody knows I am.
Play it. Play it, Muddy Waters.

On the seventh hour.
On the seventh day,
On the seventh month,
Seven doctors say,
"He was born with good luck, that you see."[40]
I got seven hundred dollars and don't you fuck with me.
Yeah, I'm here.
Everbody knows I'm here.
I'm your hoochie-koochie man, Baby Sister, everybody knows I'm here.[41]
You want me to play it, Baby Sister?

M: *Go head on, Pine. Go on, Baby. Work out.*

J: *Yeah. What the hell is going on here?*

P: *One more time, Baby Sister.*

BS: *I don't need it now.*

P: *What's that, Baby?*

BS: *Be sweet, Angel, 'cause I love you.*

P: *Is that so?*

BS: *Sugar supposed to be sweet, but ain't nothing sweeter than you.*

P: *Everybody know I'm here!*

⌗⌗⌗

P: *Now listen, buddies. My woman done messed me up.*

You got bad blood, Baby, I believe you needs a shot.
You got bad blood, I believe you needs a shot.
I said turn around here, Baby, let me see what else you got.

Love your way of loving, Baby, and your skin is nice and soft.
Love your way of loving, Baby, and your skin is nice and soft.
If you don't quit that jumping, Baby, you gonner break my needle off.
F: *Work out, Pine.*
J: *Go head and play it.*

My needle's in you, Baby, and you seem to feel all right.
My needle's in you, Baby, and you seem to feel all right.
Now when your medicine go to coming down, Baby Sister, I want you to hug me tight.
Bad Blues![42]
F: *Play the blues, Pine.*
P: *That come from Walter Davis.*

♯♯♯

J: *It's old blues but it feels good.*
F: *Work out, Pine.*

I wants to know, I wants to know, I just got to know.
F: *What you want to know?*
Why you always play around.
I wonder if you got that same feeling for me.
Baby Sister, why don't you settle down?
J: *You ain't treating her right at night.*
I wants to know, I wants to know, I just got to know.
Looks like you got me fucking.
If I'm wrong, please tell me why.
M: *You ain't wrong.*
I knows I'm out in the dark alone.
I wants to know, I wants to know, I just got to know.
Play the blues.

Floyd Thomas.

Wallace "Pine Top" Johnson.

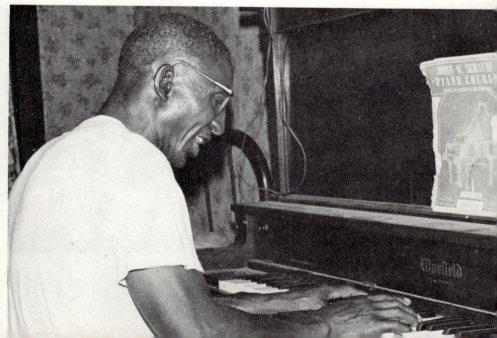

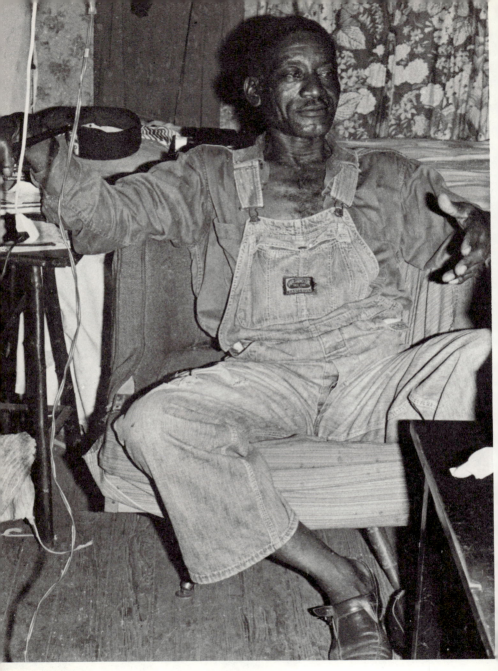

Jasper Love.

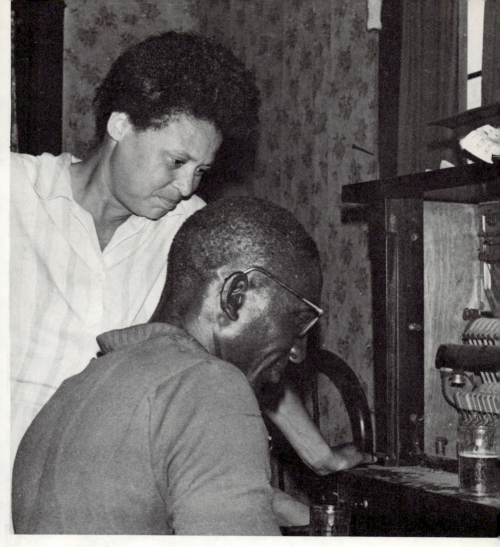

Maudie Shirley and Pine Top.

"I love you, Baby." "Do you really, Darling?"

A FINAL VIEW

Grave markers.

Row houses.

Shotgun house.

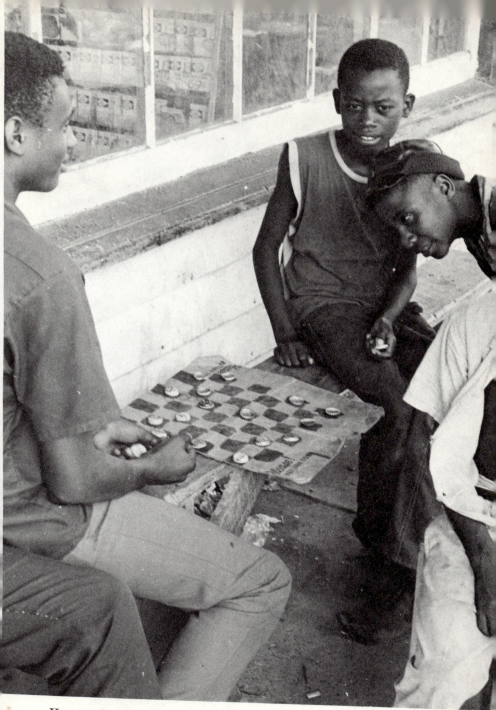

Homemade checkers.

Egremont grocery.

One-room country shack.

You used to prove that you loved me.
You used to prove every word you say.
: looks like from your ways I believe you gonner put me
n.

ats to know, I wants to know, I just got to know.

: like you got me fucking.
n wrong, please tell me.
he girls will use you now.
ow I been in trouble, but some day I will see the light.
ants to know, I wants to know, I just got to know.
e more time!

❋❋❋

That's the blues, boys. Baby Sister, is you Caledonia?
: *Hell yes, I'm Caledonia.*
n going with my baby, she got great big feet.
he long-legged and tall, and ain't had a bite to eat.
ut she's my woman and I love her just the same.
'm crazy bout you, Caledonia is your name.

Say, Love. You know what my momma told me?
She said "You know that woman called 'Caledonia'?
"I want you to leave that woman alone."
I said "Look here, Momma.
"You don't know what Caledonia putting down.
"I'm going down to her house and I'm gonner talk with her one
more time."

I believe I'll call her up.
"Caledonia, what makes your big head so hard?
"Caledonia, Caledonia.
"I'm crazy bout you, Caledonia is your name."
Gonner wrap it up now.
Good bye.[43]

❋❋❋

[Maudie suggested we all go over to her house and play some of
the tapes for her children. Pine Top, Floyd, Jasper, Baby Sister,

and I followed Maudie to her home. Her two boys, ten and twelve years old, were still awake. As they listened to the tape, they recited the dozens and toasts their mother had recorded and sang the blues lyrics with her. Then she put them in bed and sang the following prayer.]

Now I lay me down to sleep.
I pray the Lord my soul to keep.
If I should die before I wake,
I'll pray the Lord my soul to take.
And I say, Jesus, hold me.
Please hold me in thy loving arms.
But that's all right, Boys.

You saw me crying in the chapel.
The tears I shed was tears of joy.
I know the meaning of contentment.
Now I'm happy with my Lord.

Just a plain and simple chapel,
Where the people go to pray.
I pray the Lord that I grow stronger,
As I live from day to day.[44]

P: *Good night, boys.*
M: *Good night, boys. See you later. That's a song I made up for my kids. I sings it for them and nobody else. Now when they go to bed, I sing it to them. Just like a lot of people say, "Now I lay me down to sleep. I pray the Lord my soul to keep." I don't say it. I sing it to them.*

IV   LETTERS

Letters

Eight years have passed since I first recorded and photographed in the Delta. One can no longer visit Poppa Jazz's home on Saturday night or walk with Jasper Love through the Brickyard, and it seems appropriate to reflect on how the musicians' lives have changed.

Jasper Love, Sonny Boy Watson, and Lee Kizart have all moved from the Delta. In their letters (reproductions of which appear at the end of this section), they sometimes reminisce about sessions we shared together. Jasper Love moved his family north to Memphis and found a job with Orgill Brothers. He wrote inviting me up for a visit.

> send me some of that 100 proof up here so that I can get rid of these pains. . . . I'm working harder here than I was in Mississippi. My wife is getting fat and ugly and my kids are going to school everyday hollering give me a dollar. (smile). I'll close for now but hope to hear and see you in the future.

Sonny Boy Watson now lives in Las Vegas and works as a chef in a large hotel. Like Jasper, he misses the blues family and promises to return to Mississippi.

> i am living in Las Vegas . . . for a while and i will come back to Mississippi. . . . Bill i often thinks about the good time We have had together so smile and be good and gave my love to all the famiely hope to see you soon all from a dear friend.

Lee Kizart moved to Dallas in 1967, just after I recorded him in Tutwiler. He joined his son, who is also a musician, and wrote a short letter asking for photographs. My last letter to him was returned with the envelope stamped "Addressee Unknown."

As I worked on an earlier study of Delta blues, musicians followed its progress closely and were anxious to get copies for their friends. Before its publication Sonny Boy Watson wrote:

> Bill when you receve the books that you are Writing dont for get to send me one, oh yes i hope you will have good luck in all that you are dooing.

In 1970 the book was published in London and I mailed copies to all the musicians. When I later visited their homes, the books were either badly worn or had disappeared into the hands of neighbors. Jasper Love wrote:

> I enjoyed the copy that you sent, although I haven't had a chance to read it, because my family hasn't given me a chance, everytime I wants it some of them has it.

James Thomas wrote from Leland that he and his friends in Kent's Alley all enjoyed it.

> Just few line to let you no I got my booke We all was glade to get it Bill.

Because of pains in his back Thomas quit his job as a gravedigger and began working at Hewitt's Furniture Store on Main Street. He wrote more often than other musicians and relayed a story from Kent's Alley about a stranger who threatened Tobe with his life unless he gave him three thousand dollars.

> Someone called Tobe and [told] him that he had to have $3,000 about 3 o'clock he went to the police station to get a gun. The police asked him did he have one. Tobe said that he might have one that would shoot. Jazz is doing fine and also little Son.

Thomas wrote about Tobe's problem in 1970, the year Poppa Jazz's home was destroyed to make room for a parking lot. Jazz moved two blocks north into a smaller house on Kent's Alley, and the Saturday night session shifted from Kent's Alley to "Big Doug's" Cafe on Main Street.

After Little Son Jefferson's death in 1972, James Thomas and Gussie Tobe would visit Poppa Jazz in the evening to talk and sing in his small front room. The circle of musicians narrowed again this past fall when Poppa Jazz and Tobe died.

This spring James Thomas called me one morning at daybreak, and we talked about Jazz and his friends in Kent's Alley. He reminded me of their closing verse at Jazz's place.

> Good bye, Everybody.
> You know we got to go.
> Good bye, Everybody.
> People, you know we got to go.
> But if you come back to Mr. Shelby's place,
> You will see the same old show.

Letters

Hello Bill I wood like
for you to seene me
them picture I wood
like very much to
have ano all them
This is my phone number

HA10292 from Lee
to Bill

420 McKinley Street
Clarksdale, Mississippi
October 20, 1968

Dear Mr. Ferris,

Your letter found me and
my family well at the present and
hope all's well your way. We really
enjoyed your visit while you were
here.

I gave Pine Top the picture.
If you have an extra copy of the
picture send me one. If you can
I would like it very much for
you to send me an album of
the recording or send me a record.

My wife say she enjoyed you
very much while you were here
and would like for you to send
her one of the pictures of the children. Wade say that he was glad to
know that you were thinking of
him and looking for the books.
Answer when time permits.

          Sincerely yours

           Jasper & family

420 McKinley Street
Clarksdale, Mississippi
October 20, 1968

Dear Mr. Ferris,

Your letter found me and
my family well at the present and
hope all is well your way. We really
enjoyed your visit while you were
here.

I gave Pine Top the picture.
If you have an extra copy of the
picture send me one. If you can
I would like it very much for
you to send me an album of
the recording or send me a record.

My wife say she enjoyed you
very much while you were here
and would like for you to send
her one of the picture of the child
ren. Wade say that he was glad to
know that you were thinking of
him and looking for the books.
Answer when time permits.

Sincerely yours
Jasper + family

January 26, 1971
6-East Dempster
Memphis, Tennessee
38109

Hi Dr. Ferris,

How's life treating you and family?
Fine I truly hope. I enjoyed the copy
that you sent, although I haven't had
a chance to read it, because my family
hasn't given me a chance, everytime
I wants it some of them has it.

While you're Dr. Ferris send me some
of that 100 proof up here so that I
can get rid of these pains. I like to
not have known who you was in those
overalls and pipe stuck in your mouth [refers to Tom Dumas
photo]. (smile). I'm working harder here than
I was in Mississippi. My wife is getting
fat and ugly and my kids are going to
school everyday hollering give me a dollar.
(smile). I'll close for now but hope to hear
hear and see you in the future.

A friend

Jasper Love

January 26, 1971
6 East Dempster
Memphis, Tennessee
38169

Hi Dr. Ferris,

How's life treating you and family?
Fine I truly hope. I enjoyed the copy
that you sent, although I haven't had
a chance to read it, because my family
hasn't given me a chance, everytime
I wants it some of them has it.

While you're Dr. Ferris send me some
of that :00 proof up here so that I
can get rid of these pains. I like to
not have known who you was in those
overalls and pipe stuck in your mouth.
(smile). I'm working harder here than
I was in Mississippi. My wife is getting
fat and ugy and my kids are going to
school everyday hollering give me a dollar.
(smile). I'll close for now but hope to
hear and see you in the future.

A friend
Jasper Love

9-7-69
1309 Gold St
Las Vegas Nevada

Hello Bill and famiely this come to let you
here from me, yes bill i have move now
i am living in las Vegas fro now i am
going to live here for a while and i will
come back to Mississippi
Bill I am well and hope when this
letter reach you and your wife joe
i hope it will find you all well allso

Bill when you receve the books that
you are Writing dont for get to
send me one, oh yes i hope you
will have good luck in all that you
are dooing
Bill i often thinks about the good time
We have had together so smile
and be good and gave my love
to all the famiely hope to see
you soon all from a dear friend

J. W. Watson

Nick Name Sunny Boy

9-7-69
1309 Gold St
Los Vegas Nevada 89106

Hello Bill and famiely this Come to let you
here from me; yes bill i have Move now.
i am living in los Vegas for now i am
going to I live here for a While and i Will
Come back to Mississippi
Bill i am Well and hope When this
letter Reach you and your Wife joe
i hope it Will find you all Well I allso

Bill When you regene the books that
you are Writing dont for get to
send me one, oh yes i hope you
Will have good luck in all that you
are doving
Bill i often thinks about the good time
We have had togather so Smile
and be good and gaul My love
to all the famiely hope to see
you soon all from a Dear friend
J. W. Watson

Nick name Sunny Boy

29-Oct-1969
1309-Gold St
Las Vegas Nevada
Zip 89106

Hello Bill, my dear friend this is to let
you here from me i am well and hope the
same to you and your famiely and say
hello to joe and i hope to see you all
soon.
It is getting cold here now yes i know
you all bout having some cool weather
there too.
Bill i often thinks of you all i just
love to meet good peoples you know you cant find a friend any where
so i be all ways glad to here from you
Oh yes about the trip to Memphis
Man we had an exciting time boy it
was something there man the girls
just went crazy over me and son
son really played that guitar the
peoples did like it they say they

(1)

29-Oct-1969
1309- Gold St
Los Vegas Nevada
Zip 89106

Hello Bill, My dear friend this is to let
you here from me i am well and hope the
same to you and your family and say
hello to foer ont i hope to see yovall
soon.
It is getting cold here now yes i know
yovall bout having some. cool weather
there too.

Bill i often thinks of yovall i just
love to meet good peoples you koa know
ou you cant find a friend any where
so i be all ways glad to here from you.
Oh yes about the trip to Memphis
Man we hade on exciting time boy it
was somthing there Man the girls
just went Crazy over me and son
son really play that guitar the
peoples did like it they say they

①

could have listing to us all night
yes we had lots of fun.
I wrote son a letter monday to see
how he and his famiely douing, oh
yes did you go up to son like you
said if you did i know you hade
a lots of fun, so i close for now
answer soon so i will know
how you all are getting along
hope we will meet again soon
all from a true friend.

                    J. W. Watson

                    (Sonny boy)

                        (2)

could have listing to us all Night
yes we had lots of fun.
I wrote son a letter monday to see
how he and his famiely doing, oh
yes did you go up to son like you
said if you did i know you had
a lots of fun, so i close for now
answer soon so i will know
how youall are getting along.
hope we will meet again soon
all from a true friend
J. W. Watson

(Sonny boy)

②

Leland Miss
1970

Dear Bill Just a few line to
   let you no i got my booke
We all was glade to get
it Bill tehy how bleue that i
could trust if you move to a
nother camp write me let me no
i will be glad when [you] get out off
army i am still amking different thing
   Sonny Boy dont write me now
i wrot hem a letter to his
old air dress i hop he get
it bell i will write more next
time i cant write to good

       James Thomas
   720 HUDDLSTON ST
   LELAND MISS

Leland Miss.
1970

Dear Bill Just few line to
let you no got My Books
We all Wer glade to get
it Bill tey now Blue that i
Coud tret if you move to a
nether Camp write Me let Me no
i Will Be glad When get out off
army i am 2 tell More Defing thing
Jimmy Boy Dont Write Me now
i Wrot her a letter to hir
old air dress i puT he get
it Bell i Will Write More Next
time i cant Write to good
James Thomas
720 HUDDLSTON St
LELAND MiSS

720 Huddleston Street
Leland, Mississippi
Dec. 8, 1970

Dear Bill,

How are you? Well the family
is doing fine. Well, I am glad you
have good news because that's what
I want to hear. If nothing happens and you
be able to come and pick me up it
will be fine. I have made a head [sculpture]
and I am going to have a picture
made and send it to you in the next
letter. Will you and Josette be here
for Christmas. All the children say
Hello and be sure to tell Josette
Hello also. Ninnie say send her
something. Someone called Tobe and
[told] him that he had to have $3,000
about 3 o'clock he went to the
police station to get a gun. The
police asked him did he have one.
Tobe said that he might have one
that would shoot. Jazz is doing
fine and also little Son.

Sincerely

James & Family

(Written by Earlie Mae "Ninnie" Thomas)

120 Huddleston Street
Leland, Mississippi
Dec 8, 1970

Dear Brill,

How are you? Well the family is doing fine. Well, I am glad you have good news because that is what I want to hear. If nothing happens and you be able to come and pick me up it will be fine. I have made a head and I am going to have a pictured made and send it to you in the next letter. Will you and Rosette be here for Christmas. All the children say Hello and be sure to tell Rosette Hello also. Minnie say send her something. Someone called Zobe and him that he had to have $3.00 about 3 o'clock he went to the police station to get a gun. The police asked him did he have one, Zobe said that he might have one thats would shoot. Jazz is doing fine and also little Son.

Sincerely
Romeos Family

Notes

I. BLUES ROOTS

1. Rupert B. Vance, *Human Factors in Cotton Culture* (Chapel Hill: University of North Carolina Press, 1929), p. 266. The white planter's view is presented in a study by William Alexander Percy, *Lanterns on the Levee* (New York: Alfred A. Knopf, 1941). Eudora Welty captures Percy's world through fiction in *Delta Wedding* (New York: Harcourt, Brace & World, 1946). Other important white accounts of the Delta are David L. Cohn, *Where I Was Born and Raised* (Notre Dame: University of Notre Dame Press, 1967); Hodding Carter, *First Person Rural* (New York: Doubleday, 1963); and Willie Morris, *Yazoo* (New York: Harper & Row, 1971). Brief descriptions of the Delta region are in *Mississippi: A Guide to the Magnolia State* (New York: Hastings House, 1959), pp. 406–21; and *A History of Mississippi*, ed. Richard Aubrey McLemore (Hattiesburg, Miss.: University and College Press of Mississippi, 1973), pp. 8, 16, 461–70, 510, 556. Audubon describes the Delta before it was cleared in Donald Culross Peattie, ed., *The Narrative and Experiences of John James Audubon* (Boston: Houghton Mifflin Company, 1940), pp. 73–78, 149–50.

2. An excellent account of how blacks cleared and farmed the land is Frank J. Welch, "The Plantation Economy As It Relates to Land Tenure in Mississippi" (Ph.D. diss., University of Wisconsin, 1943), pp. 63–77.

3. Jasper Love, Clarksdale, Miss., 1968. This quotation and all which follow—unless noted otherwise—are transcribed field recordings taped in Mississippi during the past eight years. Musicians and their location are identified after each quotation unless the speaker preferred to remain anonymous.

4. Jasper Love, Clarksdale, Miss. Jasper Love's friend, Wade Walton, tells a similar story in Paul Oliver's *Conversations with the Blues* (New York: Horizon Press, 1965), pp. 30–32. Bukka White tells another version in *Sing Out*, vol. 18, no. 4, October–November 1968, p. 45.

5. *Report of the National Advisory Commission on Civil Disorders* (New York: New York Times, 1968), p. 240. The migration began well before

1940 and letters like the following were often received by the Chicago *Defender:*

Jackson, Miss, May the first, 1917

Sir: I was looking over the Chicago Defender and seen ad for labers both women an men it is a great lots of us woud come at once if we was only abel but we is not able but if you will send me a pas for 25 women and men I will send them north at once men and women.

This and many other letters to the Chicago *Defender* were collected and published by Emmett J. Scott, "Letters of Negro Migrants of 1916–1918," *Journal of Negro History* 4 (July 1919): 290–340. An important survey of this migration is Gunnar Myrdal, *An American Dilemma,* 2 vols. (New York: Harper & Brothers, 1964, pp. 188–96, 279–80, 329–30, 386–88.

6. Shelby Brown, Leland, Miss., 1974. X680 Jokes Concerning Various Cities. (Folklore motif number). Folklore motifs are personages, incidents, actions, or occurrences that reappear in folk tales. Folklorists have categorized and numbered these motifs in bibliographies which list where they have been collected. This and other motif numbers which follow are taken from Stith Thompson's *Motif-Index of Folk Literature,* rev. ed., 6 vols. (Bloomington, Ind.: Indiana U. Press, 1955–58), and Ernest W. Baughman's *Types and Motif-Index of the Folktales of England and North America* (The Hague: Mouton & Co., 1966) Baughman motif numbers are preceded by an asterisk.

7. An important study of the Chinese community in Mississippi is Jim Loewen, *The Mississippi Chinese: Between Black and White* (Cambridge: Harvard University Press, 1971).

8. Jasper Love, Clarksdale, Miss., 1968.

9. W. C. Handy, *Father of the Blues,* p. 87. (New York: Collier Books, 1970).

10. The history of these recordings is outlined in Robert Dixon and John Godrich, *Recording the Blues* (New York: Stein and Day, 1970). Paul Oliver describes the singers' lives in *The Story of the Blues* (New York: Chilton Book Co., 1969).

11. George Carney, a cultural geographer at Oklahoma State University, has done important research which shows how folk music traditions are linked to regions such as the Delta. An excellent introduction to this question is Wilbur Zelinsky, *The Cultural Geography of the United States* (Englewood Cliffs: Prentice-Hall, 1973).

12. David Evans discusses the influence of Speir in *Tommy Johnson* (London: Studio Vista, 1971), pp. 45–48. Evans further discusses Speir in "An Interview with H. C. Speir," *John Edwards Memorial Foundation Quarterly,* vol. 8 (1972), pp. 117–21.

13. Jasper Love, Clarksdale, Miss., 1968.

14. James "Jabo" Collins, Como, Miss., 1967. Louisiana Red recorded an earlier version in 1962 as "Red's Dream" (Roulette 4469 LP 25200).

15. Problems of "social etiquette" are discussed by Bertram W. Doyle in *The Etiquette of Race Relations in the South* (Chicago: University of Chicago Press, 1937 [Reprinted by Schocken Books, New York, 1971]), pp. vxiii–xix.

16. Anonymous speaker. Earlier Mississippi studies which encountered similar racial problems are: Newbell Niles Puckett, *The Magic and Folk Beliefs of the Southern Negro* (New York: Dover Publications, 1968), p. xxiii; John Dollard, *Caste and Class in a Southern Town* (New York: Doubleday, 1949), pp. 32–40; Samuel C. Adams, Jr., "Changing Negro Life in the Delta" (M. A. thesis, Fisk University, 1947), pp. 5–6; and Allison Davis, Burleigh B. Gardner, and Mary R. Gardner, *Deep South* (Chicago: University of Chicago Press, 1965), p. 15–18. James Agee describes a similar introduction in "Late Sunday Morning," *Let Us Now Praise Famous Men* (New York: Ballantine Books, 1972), pp. 25–30.

17. The dynamics of working in black communities are discussed by Roger D. Abrahams, *Deep Down in the Jungle* (Chicago: Aldine Pub. Co., 1970), pp. 16–38; Elliot Liebow, *Tally's Corner* (Boston: Little, Brown & Co., 1967), pp. 3–28; Ulf Hannerz, *Soulside* (New York: Columbia University Press, 1969), pp. 201–10; and James Mason Brewer, *Worser Days and Better Times* (Chicago: University of Chicago Press, 1965), pp. 23–24.

18. The word "jook" means to play the blues or have a good time. Black slang versions are reported in Hyman E. Goldin, *Dictionary of American Underworld Lingo* (New York: Citadel Press, 1962), p. 11; Bruce Rodgers, *The Queen's Vernacular: A Gay Lexicon* (San Francisco: Straight Arrow Books, 1972), p. 88; and Lorenzo Dow Turner, *Africanisms in the Gullah Dialect* (New York: Arno Press, 1969), p. 195. The word may be derived from "yuka," which appears in the ViLi dialect in the Congo and means "to make a noise, to hit or beat." K. E. Laman, *Dictionnaire Ki-Kongo/Français* (Hants, England: Gregg Press, Ltd., 1964), vol. 2, p. 1144. David Dalby examines African roots for other musical terms such as "boogie," "jive," "jazz," and "jitterbug" in "The African Element in American English," *Rappin' and Stylin' Out*, ed. Thomas Kochman (Urbana: University of Illinois Press, 1972), pp. 170–86. See also David Dalby, "Americanisms That May Once Have Been Africanisms," *Mother Wit from the Laughing Barrel*, ed. Alan Dundes (Englewood Cliffs, N.J.: Prentice-Hall, 1973), pp. 136–40.

19. Jasper Love, Clarksdale, Miss., 1968. Z183 Symbolic Names.

20. John Vlach links the southern shotgun home with Caribbean and West African examples in "Shotgun House: An African Architectural Legacy," *Pioneer America*, 7 (Jan. 1976): 43–57. See also Paul Oliver, *The Meaning of the Blues* (New York: Collier Books, 1966), pp. 23, 273.

21. Christine Thomas, Leland, Miss., 1969.

22. James Thomas, Leland, Miss., 1968.

23. Ibid.

24. Shelby Brown, Leland, Miss., 1969.

25. Ibid., 1968.

26. Gussie Tobe, Leland, Miss., 1968. Paul Oliver discusses other blues on Ohio River disasters in *The Meaning of the Blues*, pp. 268–69.

27. B. B. King compares the blues audience which gathered around the singer to a family.

> Whenever I would sing and have these people gather around me like they did, then this seemed to me as a family. This is another thing that made the blues singer continue to go on because this is his way of crying out to people. B. B. King, New Haven, Conn., 1974.

28. James Thomas and Shelby Brown, Leland, Miss., 1968. This blues may be based on Sonny Boy Williamson's "King Biscuit Blues," which was broadcast on the radio each day from Helena, Arkansas. Big Joe Williams recorded a version on his *Traditional Blues* (Folkways FS 3820).

29. Griots are traveling African musicians whose songs preserve tribal stories and legal codes. One observer felt they resembled living "libraries by supporting among themselves successive generations of living books." Maurice Delafosse, *The Negroes of Africa* (Washington, D.C.: Associated Publishers, Inc., 1931), p. 271. Other descriptions of griots are L'Abbé P. D. Boilat, *Esquisses Sénégalaises* (Paris: Bertrand, 1853), pp. 313–15; L. J. B. Berenger-Feraud, *Les Peuplades de la Sénégambie* (Paris: Ernest Leroux, 1879), pp. 60–61; G. Gorer, *African Dances* (London: Penguin, 1935), p. 55; and Paul Oliver, *Savannah Syncopators* (London: Studio Vista, 1970), pp. 43–52.

30. Traditional blues verse.

31. Jasper Love, Clarksdale, Miss., 1968.

32. Paul Oliver discusses these themes at length in *The Meaning of the Blues*.

33. John Solomon Otto and Augustus M. Burns discuss this theme in "The Use of Race and Hillbilly Recordings as Sources for Historical Research: The Problem of Color Hierarchy Among Afro-Americans in the Early Twentieth Century," *Journal of American Folklore*, vol. 85 (1972), pp. 344–55.

34. James Thomas, Leland, Miss., 1968.

35. Pine Top Johnson and Maudie Shirley, Clarksdale, Miss., 1968.

36. Two excellent examples are Otis Redding, "Tramp," (with Carla Thomas), *The Best of Otis Redding* (ATCO 2-801), and The Soul Children, "Hearsay," *Wattstax* (STS-2-3010). Earlier examples were performed by vaudeville teams like Butterbeans & Susie, Grant & Wilson, and Memphis Minnie & Kansas Joe. John Godrich and Robert M. W. Dixon list their recordings in *Blues & Gospel Records: 1902–1942* (London: Storyville Publications, 1969), pp. 128–31 (Butterbeans & Susie), 807–9 (Grant & Wilson), and 480–83 (Memphis Minnie & Kansas Joe).

37. The best survey of these female blues singers is Derrick Stewart-Baxter, *Ma Rainey and the Classic Blues Singers* (New York: Stein and Day, 1970). For a biographical study of Bessie Smith see Chris Albertson,

Bessie (New York: Stein and Day, 1972). Shorter studies of Bessie Smith are Carman Moore, *Somebody's Angel Child* (New York: T. J. Crowell Co., 1969) and Paul Oliver, *Bessie Smith* (New York, A. S. Barnes, 1971). Samuel Shapiro examines themes in the blues of Bessie Smith in "Black Women and the Blues: The Social Content of Bessie Smith's Music," *Northwest Journal of African and Black American Studies*, vol. 1, no. 2 (Fall 1973), pp. 11–19.

38. James Thomas, Leland, Miss., 1974. The blues line Thomas refers to may be derived from Jimmie Rodgers, "Out on the Road," Chess 1519.

39. James Thomas, Leland, Miss., 1968. Mercy Dee Walton first recorded the tune in 1949 as "Lonesome Cabin Blues" (Spire 102, 11-002).

40. James Thomas, Leland, Miss., 1968.

41. W. C. Handy, *Father of the Blues* (New York: Collier Books, 1970), p. 16; William Broonzy, *Big Bill's Blues* (New York: Oak Publications, 1964), p. 54. A careful study of blacks in Mississippi during this period is Vernon Lane Wharton, *The Negro in Mississippi: 1865–1890* (New York: Harper & Row, 1965). Another study which covers the same period is Jesse Thomas Wallace, *A History of the Negroes of Mississippi from 1865 to 1890* (New York: Johnson Reprint Corp., 1970). A shorter but helpful study is Mrs. Charles C. Mosley, *The Negro in Mississippi History* (Jackson, Miss.: Hederman Brothers, 1950).

42. William Francis Allen, Charles Pickard Ware, and Lucy McKim Garrison, *Slave Songs of the United States* (New York: Oak Publications, 1965), p. xviii.

43. Fanny Kemble, *Journal of a Residence on a Georgia Plantation in 1838–1839* (New York: Knopf, 1961), pp. 128–29. Janheinz Jahn explains how similar work songs developed in Dahomey, Yoruba, Haiti, Brazil, and Trinidad in *Muntu: The New African Culture* (New York: Grove Press, 1961), pp. 223–24.

44. A careful study of prison work chants which includes interviews with prisoners and texts of their chants is Bruce Jackson, *Wake Up Dead Man* (Cambridge: Harvard University Press, 1972). An important study of conditions among black prisoners is Jesse F. Steiner and Roy M. Brown, *The North Carolina Chain Gang* (Westport, Conn.: Negro Universities Press, 1970). John and Alan Lomax made classic recordings of work chants at Parchman which John Lomax describes in *Adventures of a Ballad Hunter* (New York: Macmillan Co., 1947), pp. 123–73. Their recordings are available with accompanying notes on *Afro-American Spirituals, Work Songs, and Ballads* (Library of Congress Recording AAFS L3), *Roots of the Blues* (Atlantic 1348), and *Negro Prison Songs from the Mississippi State Penitentiary* (Tradition TLP 1020).

45. Prisoners at Camp B, Lambert, Mississippi, 1967, *Mississippi Folk Voices* (Southern Folklore Records 1). In Alan Lomax's recording of "Eighteen Hammers" on *Roots of the Blues* the same phrase, "Mud! Mud! Mud!" is used to end the chant. See also Alan Lomax, *Negro Prison Songs from the Mississippi State Penitentiary* (Tradition TLP 1020). Accents in the text are beats where hammers fell.

46. Cal Taylor, Lula Junction, Miss., 1967.

47. William Broonzy, *Big Bill's Blues*, p. 35.

48. Ibid., p. 48; Janheinz Jahn, *Muntu*, p. 221.

49. William Broonzy, *Big Bill's Blues*, p. 13; W. C. Handy, *Father of the Blues*, p. 18.

50. Folklorists have collected extensively in the Delta and important studies based on this material are Newbell Niles Puckett, *Folk Beliefs of the Southern Negro* (New York: Dover, 1969; orig. pub. 1926); Richard Dorson, *American Negro Folktales* (New York: Fawcett, 1967); and Paul Oliver, *Conversation with the Blues* (New York: Horizon Press, 1965).

51. Samuel Charters, *The Bluesmen* (New York: Oak Publications, 1967), p. 32.

52. W. C. Handy, *Father of the Blues*, p. 74. The line which struck Handy referred to Moorhead, Mississippi, where the Southern and Yazoo Delta Railroad intersect. The latter was called the "Yellow Dog" because the large initials "Y.D." were written on its engines. Handy later published the tune as the "Yellow Dog Blues."

Handy was born in Florence, Alabama, in 1873 and had little interest in Delta blues until he heard a Tutwiler musician at the age of thirty. His parents had forbidden him to play the music he later celebrated, and when he once brought a guitar home his mother and father were shocked. " 'A box,' he gasped, while my mother stood frozen. 'A guitar! One of the devil's playthings. Take it away. Take it away, I tell you. Get it out of your hands. What ever possessed you to bring a sinful thing like that into our Christian home? Take it back where it came from. You hear? Get!' " (Handy, p. 10).

53. David Evans compares the one-strand with similar African instruments in "Afro-American One-Stringed Instruments," *Western Folklore*, 29 (1971): 229–45. The one-stringed "Berimbau" is played in Brazil throughout Baía and as an important part of Afro-Brazilian folk music. Tony Talbot's film *Berimbau* (New York Films) is an excellent study of the instrument which has been converted by Brazilian performer Nana into a modern chamber instrument.

54. B. B. King, New Haven, Conn., 1975.

55. Louis Dotson, Lorman, Miss., 1967.

56. James Thomas, Leland, Miss., 1968.

57. James Thomas, Leland, Miss., 1970. Samuel "Magic Sam" Maghett grew up on a farm eight miles east of Grenada and also learned how to play the guitar by stretching strings tied to nails driven into a wall. Bill Lindemann, "Liner Notes," *West Side Soul—Magic Sam's Blues Band* (Delmark DS-615). Big Joe Williams began playing a similar instrument in Crawford which Bob Koester describes in "Liner Notes," *Piney Woods Blues: Big Joe Williams* (Delmark DL-602). Eddie "One String" Jones plays a portable version of the one-strand on his record "One String Blues" (Takoma B 1023). An excellent study of the life and music of Elmore James is Barry Pearson's "The Late Great Elmore James," *Keystone Folklore Quarterly*, 17 (Winter 1972): 162–72.

58. Gussie Tobe, Leland, Miss., 1968.

59. Shelby Brown, Leland, Miss., 1974.

60. Robert Shaw, Memphis, Tenn., 1972. Z133 Poverty Personified.

61. Michael Haralambos explores age differences of blues and soul audiences in "Soul Music and Blues: Their Meaning and Relevance in Northern United States Black Ghettos," *Afro-American Anthropology*, ed. Norman F. Whitten, Jr., and John F. Szwed (New York: The Free Press, 1970), pp. 367–83. Haralambos develops this article further in *Right On: From Blues to Soul in Black America* (London: Eddison Press, 1974).

62. Earlie Mae Thomas, Leland, Miss., 1969.

63. James Thomas, Leland, Miss., 1970.

64. Earlie Mae Thomas, Leland, Miss., 1969.

65. B. B. King, New Haven, Conn., 1974.

66. Arthur Lee Williams, Birdie, Miss., 1968.

67. Ibid.

68. Mr. Vinson, Rolling Fork, Miss., 1968.

69. Arthur Lee Williams, Birdie, Miss., 1968.

70. James Thomas, Leland, Miss., 1969.

71. Ibid.

72. Recorded by Arthur "Big Boy" Crudup in 1949 on RCA Victor-20. Crudup's recordings are listed in Mike Leadbitter and Neil Slaven, *Blues Records: January, 1943 to December, 1966* (London: Hanover Books, 1968), pp. 57–60.

73. James Thomas, Leland, Miss., 1968.

74. Arthur Lee Williams, Birdie, Miss., 1968.

75. Frank Frost, Lula, Miss., 1968. Transcribed by Marty Kluger.

II. BLUES COMPOSITION

1. Sonny Matthews, Lula, Miss., 1968.

2. James Thomas, Leland, Miss., 1968.

3. There is an extensive body of scholarship on the composition and structure of blues. Newman Ivey White notes how black singers recalled their verses in *American Negro Folk Songs* (Hatboro, Pa.: Folklore Associates, 1956), p. 26. Roger Abrahams and George Foss show how blues differ from white folk forms in *Anglo-American Folksong Style* (Englewood Cliffs, N.J.: Prentice-Hall, 1968), p. 58. Discussions of the blacks who sing ballads are included in Dorothy Scarborough, *On the Trail of Negro Folk-Songs* (Hatboro, Pa.: Folklore Associates, 1963), p. 65, and G. Malcolm Laws, Jr., *Native American Balladry* (Philadelphia: The American Folklore Society, 1964), pp. 84–85, 245–56. The non-narrative structure of blues is stressed by Richard Dorson, "Negro Folksongs in Michigan from the Repertoire of J. D. Suggs," *Folklore and Folk Music Archivist*, 9 (fall 1956): 3–43, and Paul Oliver, *Screening the Blues* (London: Studio Vista, 1968), pp. 17–148. Albert Lord's concept of formulaic composition in oral epic has

been widely used in recent studies of blues. Lord defines his idea in *The Singer of Tales* (New York: Atheneum, 1965), pp. 3–12. D. K. Wilgus was the first to suggest Lord's theory related to the study of blues in his "Review of Lord's *Singer of Tales*," *Kentucky Folklore Record*, 7 (Jan.–March 1961): 40–44. Bruce Jackson applies Lord's theory in studying black song style in the Foreword of Newman Ivey White, *American Negro Folk-Songs*, p. xi. In his study of Tommy Johnson, David Evans relies heavily on Lord's work. "The Blues of Tommy Johnson: A Study of a Tradition" (M.A. thesis, University of California, Los Angeles, 1967), pp. 7, 71–72, 97–98.

I studied the formulaic structure of blues verses in my dissertation "Black Folklore from the Mississippi Delta" (Ph.D. diss., University of Pennsylvania, 1969), pp. 304–473. David Evans has done important recent work on blues composition in "Tradition and Creativity in the Folk Blues" (Ph.D. diss., University of California, Los Angeles, 1976) and in "Techniques of Blues Composition Among Black Folksingers," *Journal of American Folklore*, 87, no. 345 (July–Sept. 1974), pp. 240–49.

4. James Thomas, Leland, Miss., 1968.

5. Sonny Boy Watson, Leland, Miss., 1968.

6. James Thomas, Leland, Miss., 1968.

7. John W. Work observed a similar competition between blues singers in Nashville, Tenn. *American Negro Songs and Spirituals* (New York: Bonanza, 1940), p. 36.

8. I recorded Bessie Jones performing this verse as a children's riddle and her answer was "a child nursing its mother." Similar riddles have been recorded in the Bahamas, Italy, and Serbia. The Bahama version is: "Bellee/Han 'round de back,/Take a piece o' meat/Ter fill de crack—A woman nursin' a child." Archer Taylor, *English Riddles from Oral Tradition* (Berkeley: University of California Press, 1951), p. 526. David Evans notes the line is also used as the punch line of a joke [private correspondence].

9. James Thomas and Joe Cooper, Leland, Miss., 1968.

10. Marshall and Jean Stearns discuss both the boogie and the slow drag in *Jazz Dance* (New York: Macmillan, 1968), pp. 4, 5, 13, 21, 67, 99, 108, 153, 162, 234, 299, 330, 376. Another study which deals with blues dance is Lynne Fauley Emery, *Black Dance* (Palo Alto, Calif.: National Press Books, 1972), p. 230.

11. David Evans develops an important discussion of blues composition and textual variation in "Techniques of Blues Composition Among Black Folksingers," *Journal of American Folklore*, 87, no. 345 (July–Sept. 1974), pp. 240–49. While verses he recorded in two performances of the same tune by "Boogie" Bill Webb were virtually the same, his earlier study of Tommy Johnson showed there was considerable textual change from performance to performance. *Tommy Johnson* (London: Studio Vista, 1972), pp. 91–94.

12. B. B. King, "Nobody Loves Me but My Mother," *Indianola Mississippi Seeds* (ABCS-713).

13. Little Milton, *Little Milton Sings Big Blues* (Checker LPS-3002).

14. Ella Mae Callion, Leland, Miss., 1974.

15. Ella Mae Callion, Leland, Miss., 1974.

16. Joe "Big Daddy" Louis, Jackson, Miss., 1974.

17. The role of Voodoo in blues is discussed by Paul Oliver in *The Meaning of the Blues* (New York: Collier Books, 1966), pp. 161–68. Newbell Niles Puckett discussed the influence of music on hoodoo in *The Magic and Folk Beliefs of the Southern Negro*, pp. 56–57, 537, 570. A monumental collection of hoodoo lore is Harry Middleton Hyatt, *Hoodo-Conjuration-Witchcraft-Rootwork*, 4 vols. (Hannibal, Mo.; Cambridge, Md.: Western Publishing Co., 1970, 1973, 1974).

18. Jelly Jaw Short, "Snake Doctor Blues," *St. Louis Town 1929–1933* (Yazoo Records L 1003). For a complete discography of Short's original recordings, see John Godrich and Robert M. W. Dixon, *Blues & Gospel Records: 1902–1942* (London: Storyville Publications, 1969), p. 612. D1531.8 Witch Flies with Aid of Word Charm.

19. Zora Hurston, *Voodoo Gods* (London: J. M. Dent & Sons, 1938), pp. 122–25, 260. Maya Deren, *Divine Horsemen* (New York: Chelsea House, 1970), pp. 114–25. G303.10.3 Snake as Follower of the Devil.

20. Tony Hollins recorded "Crawling Kingsnake Blues" in 1941 and John Lee Hooker reissued the song in 1959, "Crawling Kingsnake Blues" (Vee Jay 331, LP 1007, 1049). I discuss images of snakes which appear in the blues, folktales, and sculpture of James Thomas in "Vision of Afro-American Folk Art: The Sculpture of James Thomas," *Journal of American Folklore*, 88 (April–June 1975): 115–31. Robert Thompson shows how widespread the snake motif is in Afro-American folk sculpture in "African Influence on the Art of the United States," in *Black Studies in the University*, ed. Armstead L. Robinson, Craig C. Foster, and Donald H. Ogilvie (New Haven: Yale University Press, 1969), pp. 159–67. Paul Garon discusses snakes in the blues in *Blues and the Poetic Spirit* (London: Eddison, 1975).

21. Newbell Niles Puckett, *The Magic and Folk Beliefs of the Southern Negro*, p. 299. D967 Magic Roots.

22. Muddy Waters, "Hoochie Koochie Man," *Muddy Waters: Sail On* (Chess 1539). See also Leadbitter and Slaven, *Blues Records*, pp. 248–55. Puckett discusses the black cat bone and John the Conqueror Root in *Magic and Folk Beliefs of the Southern Negro*, pp. 193, 255–56, 299. Numerous references appear in each of Harry Hyatt's four volumes of *Hoodoo-Conjuration-Witchcraft-Rootwork*.

23. Walter Davis, "Root Doctor Blues," *Think You Need a Shot* (RCA International INT 1085). See also Godrich and Dixon, *Blues and Gospel Records*, p. 187. D1181 Magic Needle.

24. Paul Oliver, *Screening the Blues* (London: Cassell, 1968), pp. 189–90.

25. Wallace "Pine Top" Johnson, Clarksdale, Miss., 1968. Walter Davis recorded an earlier version entitled "Think You Need a Shot" (Bluebird B. 6498) April 3, 1936. Paul Oliver discusses Davis's version and others by Jimmy Gordon, Brownie McGhee, and Champion Jack Dupree in *Screening the Blues*, pp. 189–90.

26. James Thomas, Leland, Miss., 1968. Paul Oliver discusses the relation between blues and religion in *Screening the Blues,* pp. 44–89. Other important discussions are in Charles Keil, *Urban Blues* (Chicago: University of Chicago Press, 1967), pp. 143–63, and Albert Murray, *Stomping the Blues* (New York: McGraw-Hill, 1976), pp. 21–42.

27. William "Sonny" Matthews, Lula, Miss., 1967.

28. Amanda Gordon, Rose Hill, Miss., 1962. A good example of a hymn which is expanded to fit the religious service is "Ring the Bell, I Done Got Over." During the baptizings in the Rose Hill community, Amanda Gordon leads her congregation in singing the hymn while the convert is led out of the water. I recorded one version of the hymn with eighteen verses in a performance which lasted over ten minutes. Amanda Gordon, Rose Hill, Miss., 1963.

29. Arthur Lee Williams, Birdie, Miss., 1968.

30. James Thomas, Leland, Miss., 1969.

31. Lee Kizart, Tutwiler, Miss., 1967. Q391 Punishment for Singing Worldly Songs.

32. Ibid.

33. Arthur Vinson, Rolling Fork, Miss., 1967. *G303.25.23* The Devil and Music.

34. James Thomas, Leland, Miss., 1968.

35. Arthur Vinson, Rolling Fork, Miss., 1967.

36. Lee Kizart, Tutwiler, Miss., 1967.

37. James Thomas, Leland, Miss., 1973. G303.8.3.1. Devil Is Thrust into Hell by God.

38. Ibid.

39. F81.1.2. Journey to Land of Dead to Visit Deceased.

40. G303.9.4. The Devil as a Tempter.

41. G303.9.4. The Devil as a Tempter.

42. Shelby Brown, Leland, Miss., 1968.

43. James Thomas, Leland, Miss., 1968.

44. Ibid.

45. Anonymous quote in Samuel C. Adams, Jr., "Changing Negro Life in the Delta," (M.S. thesis, Fisk University, 1947), p. 75.

46. James Thomas, Leland, Miss., 1968.

47. The following list of recorded songs indicates their titles and possible sources. Sources acknowledged by Thomas are italicized.

Cairo	(Little Son Jackson)
Boogie Till the Break of Day	(John Lee Hooker)
Bull Cow Blues	(*Texas Slim* from Yazoo City, Miss. Recorded also by Charlie Patton and Big Bill Broonzy)
Devil Blues	(*Composed by Thomas.* Recorded also by Skip James and Jack Owens)
How Long Is My Baby Been Gone	(*Junior Parker*)
I Wanta Be Your Man	(two versions)

What Is This Keep on Worrying Me	(Blind Lemon Jefferson)
Deep Sea Blues	(Tommy McClennan)
Baby Please (Don't Go)	(Big Joe Williams)
Good Morning, Little School Girl	(*Sonny Boy Williamson*)
Bottle 'Em Up and Go	(Tommy McClennan)
I Once Was a Gambler	(*Little Son Jackson*)
Rock Me, Momma	(Arthur "Big Boy" Crudup and Little Son Jackson)
Forty-Four Blues	(Little Brother Montgomery, Roosevelt Sykes)
Boogie Woogie	(instrumental)
Little Red Shoes	(*Eddie Collins,* his grandfather)
Ethel Mae	(*Arthur "Big Boy" Crudup*)
Got No Place to Go	(Howlin' Wolf)
Come On, Baby, Take a Walk with Me	(Robert Junior Lockwood)
I Was Standing at the Crossroads	(*Elmore James,* Robert Johnson)
Train Blues	(guitar instrumental with harp led by Little Son Jefferson)
Fox Hunt	(guitar instrumental with harp led by Little Son Jefferson)
Smoky Mountain Blues	(Leroy Carr, Memphis Eddie Pee)
Ain't Going Down That Long Lonesome Road	(Howlin' Wolf)
Shake 'Em On Down	(Bukka White)
Momma, Talk to Your Daughter	(J. B. Lenoir)
Life Is Just Only a Dream	(two versions)
Cried So Much for You	
I Once Had a Girl, She Waddn't but Sixteen Years Old	(Muddy Waters)
Been So Long Blues	
I Got Something to Tell You	

48. Scott Dunbar, Lake Mary, Miss., 1967.

49. Celeste Dunbar, Lake Mary, Miss., 1967.

50. Audience is a strong influence on the following repertoire which Dunbar performs for whites at Lake Mary.

Blues	*White*
Baby, Who Been Fooling with You (Sleepy John Estes)	Just Because
Sweet Rolling Momma	That's All Right, Momma (Elvis Presley version)
Don't Deny My Name	
Forty-Four Blues (Little Brother Montgomery, Roosevelt Sykes)	Put On the Old Gray Bonnet
Momma, Don't You Lay It on Me	*Down by the Riverside
It's So Cold Up North	Old Hen Cackle
Big Fat Momma (Tommy Johnson)	Little Liza Jane

Baby Please Don't Go (Big Joe Williams)

Bottle 'Em Up and Go (Tommy McClennan)

Poppa Crump (instrumental)

Shake 'Em On Down (Bukka White)

Sally Goodin

That's My Baby

*Swing Low, Sweet Chariot

Wabash Cannonball

*We Shall Wear That Crown In Glory

I Am Thinking Tonight of My Blue Eyes

She'll Be Coming Around the Mountain

You Are My Sunshine

My Blue Heaven

Careless Love

*Sweet Home

It's a Sin I Love You So

Lindy Cindy

Tennessee Waltz

Good Night, Irene

Good Bye, My Darling, Good Bye

*I Stretched My Hand to Thee

Went to See My Darling Last Night

[Note: Songs marked with an asterisk (*) in the "White" column are traditional black pieces sung in a white style.]

David Evans points out that "Sally Goodin," "Old Hen Cackle," and "Little Liza Jane" are fiddle tunes which have possible black origins [private correspondence]. They are played by Dunbar in a white country style.

51. Tony Russell shows how black and white musicians have shared similar musical traditions in *Blacks, Whites, and Blues* (New York: Stein and Day, 1970). Two white Delta singers who have recorded blues are Mose Allison and Sid Selvidge. Allison can be heard on *I Don't Worry About a Thing* (Atlantic 1389), *Swingin' Machine* (Atlantic 1398), *The Word from Mose* (Atlantic 1424), *Mose Alive!* (Atlantic 1450), and *Wild Man on the Loose* (Atlantic 1456). Selvidge just released *The Cold of the Morning* (Peabody P5101). Joe Dan Boyd presents an excellent history of black Sacred Harp tradition in northeastern Mississippi in "Negro Sacred Harp Songsters in Mississippi," *Mississippi Folklore Register*, 5, no. 3 (Fall 1971), pp. 60–83.

52. Tom Dumas, Tutwiler, Miss., 1967.

53. Tom Dumas, Tutwiler, Miss., 1967.

54. Tom Dumas, Tutwiler, Miss., 1967. "Country" Charley Pride is also from the Delta, and his life offers an interesting parallel to the experience of Dumas. His childhood in Sledge and unique success as a black country singer are presented by Ann Malone in "Charley Pride," *Stars of Country Music*, ed. Bill C. Malone and Judith McCulloh (Urbana: University of Illinois Press, 1975), pp. 340–56.

III. BLUES HOUSE PARTY

1. Zora Neale Hurston describes a similar scene in Florida in *Mules and Men* (New York: Harper & Row, 1970), pp. 220–27.

2. James Thomas, Leland, Miss., 1969.

3. Lee Kizart, Tutwiler, Miss., 1967.

4. W. C. Handy emphasizes how Delta musicians used music to avoid violence at dances in *Father of the Blues*, p. 89.

5. "Toasts" are lengthy performances of rhymed narratives which are often set in an urban context such as a barroom. Excellent texts of toasts are in Roger Abrahams, *Deep Down in the Jungle* (Chicago: Aldine Pub. Co., 1970), and Bruce Jackson, *Get Your Ass in the Water and Swim Like Me* (Cambridge: Harvard University Press, 1974). The "dozens" are two-line rhymed insults directed at female members of another person's family. Extensive texts are included in *Deep Down in the Jungle* and in William Labov, *Language in the Inner City* (Philadelphia: University of Pennsylvania Press, 1972). Paul Oliver discusses the use of dozens and toasts in the blues in "The Blue Blues: The Collector as Censor," *Screening the Blues* (London: Cassell, 1968), pp. 164–81.

6. A variant of the line from "East Chicago Blues" was recorded by Pine Top and Lindberg on Victor 23330 and refers to a massacre of blacks in East St. Louis in July 1917. Paul Oliver discusses its history in *The Meaning of the Blues*, p. 206.

7. Clarence "Pine Top" Smith, "Pine Top's Boogie Woogie" (Vocalion 1245), recorded in Chicago December 29, 1928. I am indebted to David Evans and Frank Scott for references to most of the recorded versions of blues performed in this session. For further information on recordings and singers see both Mike Leadbitter and Neil Slaven, *Blues Records: 1943–1966* and J. Godrich and R. M. W. Dixon, *Blues & Gospel Records: 1902–1942*.

8. Jimmy Rogers and His Trio, "That's All Right" (Chess 1435), recorded in Chicago, 1950. See also Othum Brown with Little Walter (harmonica), "Ora Nelle Blues" ("That's Alright"), recorded in Chicago, 1947, and Little Junior Parker, "That's Alright" (Duke 168), recorded in Houston, 1957–58.

9. A possible source is Roosevelt Sykes's "New 44 Blues" (BBB 5323, Sr. 3404), recorded in Chicago in 1933. Paul Oliver gives a history of this blues in "The Forty Fours," *Screening the Blues*, pp. 90–127.

10. Mercy Dee Walton, "One Room Country Shack" (Specialty 458), recorded in Los Angeles, 1953–54.

11. Muddy Waters, "All Night Long" (Chess 1509), recorded in Chicago, 1952; Muddy Waters, "Rock Me" (Chess 1652), recorded in Chicago, 1957. See also Arthur "Big Boy" Crudup, "Rock Me Momma" (Victor 20–29–78), recorded in Chicago, December 15, 1944, and Lil' Son

Jackson, "Rockin' and Rollin'" (Imperial LP 9142), recorded in Los Angeles, December 16, 1950.

12. *x1321.4* Remarkable Behavior of Snake.

13. Eurreal "Little Brother" Montgomery, "Vicksburg Blues" (Paramount 13006), recorded in Grafton, Wisc., c. September 1930. See also Paul Oliver, "The Forty Fours," *Screening the Blues*, pp. 90–127.

14. Miles Mark Fisher feels spirituals played a major role in communicating coded messages among slaves and carefully examines their texts in *Negro Slave Songs in the United States* (New York: Russell & Russell, 1968).

15. Robert Johnson, "I Believe I'll Dust My Broom" (Vocalion 03475, Conqueror 8871), recorded in San Antonio, Tex., November 23, 1936. A later more popular version by Elmore James, "Dust My Broom" (Trumpet 146), recorded in Jackson, Miss., 1952, was reissued several times by James.

16. Jimmy Reed, "Big Boss Man" (VJ 380), recorded in Chicago, March 29, 1960.

17. No version of the "Pine Top Boogie" by Roosevelt Sykes is listed in either Godrich and Dixon or Leadbitter and Slaven.

18. Eurreal "Little Brother" Montgomery, "Santa Fe" (BB B681), recorded in New Orleans, July 1936. See also Thunder Smith, "Santa Fe Blues," (Gold Star 644, Arhoolie 2006). Karl Gert zur Heide includes a complete text of the version by "Little Brother" Montgomery in *Deep South Piano: The Story of Little Brother Montgomery* (London: Studio Vista, 1970), p. 99. Paul Oliver shows how blues singers develop Santa Claus throughout their music in "The Santa Claus Crave," *Preaching the Blues*, pp. 26–43.

19. Lowell Fulson recorded a version of "Black Night" (Kent 431) in Los Angeles in 1965.

20. "St. Louis" Jimmy Oden, "Going Down Slow" (Bluebird B-8889, RCA Victor 20–2598), recorded in Chicago, November 11, 1941.

21. Roscoe Gordon, "Just a Little Bit" (VeeJay 332), recorded in Chicago, 1959.

22. Johnny Moore and His Three Blazers (Charles Brown, vocalist), "Drifting Blues" (Aladdin 112), recorded in Los Angeles, September 14, 1945. James "Beale Street" Clarke, "Drifting" (Victor 20–1887, Bluebird 34–0748), recorded in Chicago, February 22, 1946.

23. Jimmy Reed, "Ain't That Loving You Baby" (VJ 168), recorded in Chicago, November 9, 1955.

24. Roosevelt Sykes, "Sunny Road" (RCA Victor 20–1906), recorded in Chicago, February 18, 1946.

25. Fats Domino, "My Girl Josephine" (Imperial 5704), 1960.

26. See J. B. Lenoir, "How Much More" (JOB 1008), recorded in Chicago, 1952. Another version, "How Long—How Long Blues" (Vocalion 1191), was recorded by Leroy Carr in Indianapolis in 1928.

27. Possibly from Cecil Gant, "I Wonder" (Gilt Edge 501, Bronze 117, Star 1159, Sound 601, Decca 30320), recorded in Los Angeles, 1944–46.

28. Junior Parker, "Next Time You See Me" (Duke 164), recorded in Houston, 1956.

29. Paul Oliver calls this "The elephant stanza" and discusses its history in *Screening the Blues*, pp. 242–43. See Eddie "One-String" Jones, "The Dozens" (Takoma B 1023), recorded February 1/March 1, 1960. Newman Ivey White includes an expurgated version which H. C. Abbot recorded in Florida in 1915 in *American Negro Folk Songs* (Hatboro, Pa.: Folklore Associates, 1965), p. 136. See also Rufus "Speckled Red" Perryman, "Dirty Dozens" (Delmark DL 601), recorded in St. Louis, September 2, 1956.

30. "All Night Long." See note 11.

31. Ma Rainey, "See See Rider Blues—1" (Pm 12252), recorded in New York, 1924. A later version by Muriel "Wee Bea Booze" Nicholls is "See See Rider Blues" (Decca 8633, 48055), recorded in New York, March 26, 1942.

32. Jimmy Reed, "Ain't That Lovin' You Baby" (VeeJay 168), recorded in Chicago, December 5, 1955.

33. Z51 Claims Involving Contradictions or Extremes.

34. Commercial recordings of toasts performed on music are on *Snatch and the Poontangs* (Kent KST 557x). A series of Rudy Ray Moore includes *Eat Out More Often* (Comedians COMS 1104), *Merry Christmas, Baby* (Comedians, COMS 1108), *The Second Ruby Ray Moore Album* (Comedians COMS 1105), *Jody the Grinder* (Comedians COMS 1110).

35. Tommy McClennan, "Bottle 'Em Up and Go" (Bluebird B 8373), recorded in Chicago, November 22, 1939.

36. Leroy Carr, "How Long—How Long Blues," see note 26. This may be from one of Carr's later versions.

37. Roosevelt Sykes, "Sunny Road," see note 24.

38. Roger Abrahams discusses the dozens and their texts in *Deep Down in the Jungle*. Paul Oliver explains their role in blues in *Screening the Blues*, pp. 235–46.

39. Big Joe Williams, "Baby Please Don't Go" (Bluebird B 8969), recorded in Chicago, 1941. Reissued in 1947 (Columbia 37945), and 1958 (Delmark DL 602).

40. Z71.5 Formulistic Number: Seven.

41. McKinley "Muddy Waters" Morganfield, "Hoochie Koochie Man" (Chess LP 1427), recorded in Chicago, January 7, 1964.

42. Walter Davis, "Think You Need a Shot (the Needle)" (Bluebird B 6498), recorded in Chicago, April 3, 1936. Paul Oliver discusses this version and others by Jimmy Gordon, Brownie McGhee, and Champion Jack Dupree in *Screening the Blues*, pp. 189–90.

43. Joe Pollum, "Black Gal What Makes Your Head So Hard?" (Bluebird B 5459), recorded in San Antonio, April 3, 1934. Later issued by Louis Jordan as "Caledonia Boogie" (Decca 8670), c. 1945.

44. Elvis Presley, "Crying in the Chapel" (RCA Victor 0643), 1965.

Bibliography

Black Folklore

Blues should be viewed within the full range of Afro-American folklore. Ralph Ellison stresses that blacks are a people "of the word" rather than "of the book" and music is only part of their oral tradition. The following studies present an overview of black folklore and its expression in music, tales, and art.

Abrahams, Roger, and John F. Szwed, eds. *An Annotated Bibliography of Afro-American Folk Culture*. Philadelphia: American Folklore Society Bibliographical and Special Series (in press).

Dundes, Alan, ed. *Mother Wit from the Laughing Barrel*. Englewood Cliffs, N.J.: Prentice-Hall, 1973.

Herskovits, Melville. *The Myth of the Negro Past*. Boston: Beacon Press, 1958.

Szwed, John F., ed. *Black America*. New York: Basic Books, 1970.

Thompson, Robert. *An Aesthetic of the Cool: Black Art in Transatlantic Perspective*. New York: Harper & Row (in press).

Vansina, Jan. *Oral Tradition*. London: Routledge & Kegan Paul, 1965.

Whitten, Norman E. Jr., and John F. Szwed, eds. *Afro-American Anthropology*. New York: The Free Press, 1970.

The Church, Tales, and Hoodoo

Careful study of blues should consider how other black folk traditions such as the church, tales, and Voodoo influence the music. Singers often allude to each, and together they provide a richer frame for understanding the blues perspective.

The Church

Cone, James H. *The Spirituals and the Blues*. New York: The Seabury Press, 1972.

Fisher, Miles Mark. *Negro Slave Songs in the United States.* New York: Russell & Russell, 1968.

Heilbut, Tony. *The Gospel Sound.* New York: Simon & Schuster, 1971.

Johnson, Clifton H., ed. *God Struck Me Dead.* Boston: Pilgrim Press, 1969.

Lehmann, Theo. *Negro Spirituals.* Berlin: Eckart-Verlag, 1965.

Lovell, John Jr. *Black Song: The Forge and the Flame.* New York: Macmillan, 1972.

Rosenberg, Bruce A. *The Art of the American Folk Preacher.* New York: Oxford University Press, 1970.

Tales

Abrahams, Roger. *Deep Down in the Jungle.* Chicago: Aldine Pub. Co., 1970.

Botkin, B. A., ed. *Lay My Burden Down.* Chicago: University of Chicago Press, 1965.

Dorson, Richard. *American Negro Folktales.* New York: Fawcett, 1967.

Foster, Herbert L. *Ribbin', Jivin', and Playin' the Dozens.* Cambridge, Mass.: Ballinger Press, 1974.

Jackson, Bruce. *Get Your Ass in the Water and Swim Like Me.* Cambridge: Harvard University Press, 1974.

Kockman, Thomas, ed. *Rappin' and Stylin' Out.* Chicago: University of Illinois Press, 1972.

Labov, William. *Language in the Inner City.* Philadelphia: University of Pennsylvania Press, 1972.

Voodoo

Hurston, Zora Neale. *Mules and Men.* New York: Harper & Row, 1970.

Hyatt, Harry Middleton. *Hoodoo-Conjuration-Witchcraft-Rootworks* (4 vols.). Washington, D.C.: American University Bookstore, 1970.

Puckett, Newbell Niles. *The Magic and Folk Beliefs of the Southern Negro.* New York: Dover Publications, 1969.

Surveys of Black Music

Several studies place blues within the over-all history of black music. Eileen Southern's work is the most extensive and is accompanied by an important volume of secondary readings.

Roberts, John Storm. *Black Music of Two Worlds.* New York: Praeger, 1972.

Rublowsky, John. *Black Music in America.* New York: Basic Books, 1971.

Southern, Eileen, *The Music of Black Americans: A History.* New York: W. W. Norton, 1971.

————, ed. *Readings in Black American Music*. New York: W. W. Norton, 1971.

Walton, Ortiz M. *Music: Black, White and Blue*. New York: William Morrow, 1972.

Jazz and Blues

Writers agree there are important links between jazz and blues, but no one has fully presented both traditions in the same study. Blues scholars know little about jazz, and jazz critics usually consider blues a distant sound from which their music evolved. Blues and jazz are in fact parallel musical traditions and the best synthesis of the two is still by Marshall Stearns. Important jazz biographies are *Mister Jelly Roll* and *Music on My Mind*.

Buerkle, Jack V., and Danny Barker. *Bourbon Street Black*. New York: Oxford University Press, 1973.

Hentoff, Nat. *Jazz County*. New York: Dell, 1967.

Hodier, André. *Jazz: Its Evolution and Essence*. New York: Grove Press, 1956.

Jones, LeRoi. *Black Music*. New York: William Morrow & Co., 1968.

————. *Blues People*. New York: William Morrow & Co., 1963.

Lomax, Alan. *Mister Jelly Roll*. New York: Grosset & Dunlap, 1950.

Mezzrow, Mezz, and Bernard Wolfe. *Really the Blues*. Garden City, N.Y.: Doubleday, 1972.

Sargeant, Winthrop. *Jazz, Hot and Hybrid*. New York: Da Capo, 1975.

Schuller, Gunther. *Early Jazz*. New York; Oxford University Press, 1968.

Shapiro, Nat, and Nat Hentoff. *Hear Me Talkin' to Ya*. New York: Dover, 1966.

Smith, Willie The Lion. *Music on My Mind*. London: MacGiffon & Kee, 1965.

Stearns, Marshall. *The Story of Jazz*. New York: New American Library, 1958.

Wilmer, Valerie. *Jazz People*. London: Allison & Busby, 1970.

Roots of the Blues: History

Histories of slavery, Reconstruction, and the Jim Crow South provide an important context for understanding how blues developed. Excellent studies exist on each period, and recent work by Blassingame, Genovese, Levine, and Rawick stress the importance of oral tradition during slavery.

Blassingame, John W. *The Slave Community*. New York: Oxford University Press, 1972.

Genovese, Eugene D. *Roll Jordan Roll*. New York: Pantheon Books, 1974.

Levine, Lawrence W. *Black Culture and Black Consciousness.* New York: Oxford University Press, 1977.

Rawick, George P. *From Sundown to Sunup.* Westport, Conn.: Greenwood Pub. Co., 1972.

Wharton, Vernon Lane. *The Negro in Mississippi.* New York: Harper & Row, 1965. First published 1947.

Woodward, C. Vann. *The Strange Career of Jim Crow.* New York: Oxford University Press, 1974. First published 1954.

Woofter, T. J. Jr. *Landlord and Tenant on the Cotton Plantation.* New York: Negro Universities Press, 1969. First Published 1936.

Roots of the Blues: Music

The African griot, slave singers, and work chanters share much with the blues musician. Studies of the singers and texts of their songs help us compare each with their blues counterpart.

Allen, William Francis, Charles Pickard Ware, and Lucy McKim Garrison. *Slave Songs of the United States.* New York: Oak, 1965.

Jackson, Bruce. *Wake Up Dead Man.* Cambridge: Harvard University Press, 1972.

Oliver, Paul. *Savannah Syncopators.* New York: Stein & Day, 1970.

Parrish, Lydia. *Slave Songs of the Georgia Sea Islands.* Hatboro, Pa.: Folklore Associates, 1965.

Early Studies of Blues

Serious study of the blues based on field-recorded materials began earlier in this century. Though often edited and expurgated, this research provides an important body of texts and analysis which complements more recent work.

Courlander, Harold. *Negro Folk Music, U.S.A.* New York: Columbia University Press, 1966. First printed 1963.

Lomax, Alan. *The Folk Songs of North America.* Garden City, N.Y.: Doubleday, 1960.

Odom, Howard W., and Guy B. Johnson. *The Negro and His Songs.* New York: New American Library, 1969. First printed 1925.

Scarborough, Dorothy. *On the Trail of Negro Folk Songs.* Hatboro, Pa.: Folklore Associates, 1963. First printed 1925.

White, Newman I. *American Negro Folk Songs.* Hatboro, Pa.: Folklore Associates, 1965, First published 1928.

Blues as Literature

Writers and literary critics are increasingly interested in the blues as poetry. Its distinctive language and images are a rich resource for literary analysis.

Bluestin, Gene. *The Voice of the Folk*. Amherst: University of Massachusetts Press, 1972.

Charters, Samuel. *The Poetry of the Blues*. New York: Oak Publications, 1963.

Ellison, Ralph. *Shadow and Act*. New York: Vintage Books, 1972. First published 1953.

Garron, Paul. *Blues and the Poetic Spirit*. London: Eddison Press, 1975.

Hughes, Langston. *The Weary Blues*. New York: Knopf, 1947.

Murray, Albert. *The Hero and the Blues*. Columbia: University of Missouri Press, 1973.

———. *The Omni-Americans*. New York: Avon Books, 1970.

Blues Texts

No study of blues as literature is possible without accurately transcribed texts. Complete song texts can be found in several studies, the most comprehensive of which is *The Blues Line*.

Brown, Sterling A., Arthur P. Davis, and Ulysses Lee, eds. *The Negro Caravan*. New York: The Dryden Press, 1941.

Handy, W. C., ed. *Blues: An Anthology*. New York: Collier Books, 1972. First printed 1926.

Oster, Harry. *Living Country Blues*. Detroit, Mich.: Folklore Associates, 1969.

Sackheim, Eric. *The Blues Line: A Collection of Blues Lyrics* New York: Schirmer Books, 1975.

Work, John W. *American Negro Songs and Spirituals*. New York: Bonanza Books, 1940.

Blues Talk: Interviews

Comments by blues singers are invaluable in understanding their music. All too often writers ignore these interviews and assume performers are incapable of discussing their music. Important interviews are included in several books and in issues of the journals *Blues-Link, Blues Unlimited,* and *Living Blues*.

Blues Link, P. O. Box 152, Barnet, Herts., EN5 4HU, England.

Blues Unlimited. 8 Brondrom Road, Lewishorn, London SE 13 5EA, England.

Leadbitter, Mike. *Nothing but the Blues*. London: Hanover Books, 1971.

Living Blues. P. O. Box 11303, Chicago, Illinois 60611

Oliver, Paul. *Conversation with the Blues*. New York: Horizon Press, 1965.

Mitchell, George. *Blow My Blues Away*. Baton Rouge: Louisiana State University Press, 1971.

Neff, Robert, and Anthony Connor. *Blues*. Boston: David R. Godine, 1975.

Ramsey, Frederic Jr. *Been Here and Gone*. New Brunswick: Rutgers University Press, 1969.

Biographies

Blues biographies present performers with more care and detail than is possible in interviews. Through the biography we can place blues in the context of a singer's life and show how personal experience shapes the music. The following works range from brief profiles by Samuel Charters to detailed biographies by David Evans and Chris Albertson. The autobiographies of Big Bill Broonzy and W. C. Handy are outstanding.

Broonzy, William. *Big Bill's Blues*. New York: Oak Publications, 1964.

Charters, Samuel. *The Bluesmen*. New York: Oak Publications, 1967.

Evans, David. *Tommy Johnson*. London: Studio Vista, 1971.

Fahey, John. *Charley Patton*. London: Studio Vista, 1970.

Garon, Paul. *The Devil's Son-in-Law: The Story of Peetie Wheatstraw and His Songs*. London: Studio Vista, 1971.

Gert zur Heide, Karl. *Deep South Piano: The Story of Little Brother Montgomery*. London: Studio Vista, 1970.

Handy, W. C. *Father of the Blues*. New York: Collier Books, 1970. First published in 1941.

Stewart-Baxter, Derrick. *Ma Rainey and the Classic Blues Singers*. New York: Stein & Day, 1970.

Leadbelly

Asch, Moses, and Alan Lomax. *The Leadbelly Songbooks*. New York: Oak Publications, 1962.

Garoin, Richard M., and Edmond G. Addeo. *The Midnight Special*. New York: Bernard Geis Associates, 1971.

Lomax, John and Alan. *The Leadbelly Legend*. New York: Folkways Publishers, 1965.

————. *Negro Folk Songs as Sung by Leadbelly*. New York, 1936.

Bessie Smith

Albertson, Chris. *Bessie*. New York: Stein & Day, 1972.

Moore, Carman. *Somebody's Angel Child*. New York: T. Y. Crowell, 1969.

Oliver, Paul. *Bessie Smith*. New York: A. S. Barnes, 1971.

Blues and White Music

Black and white musicians have often shared styles to produce black country singers and white bluesmen. Studies on traditional blues, the blues revival, and country music lay the groundwork for a major history of this exchange.

Groom, Bob. *The Blues Revival*. London: Studio Vista, 1971.

Malone, Bill C. *Country Music, U.S.A.* Austin: University of Texas Press, 1968.

———, and Judith McCulloh. *Stars of Country Music*. Chicago: University of Illinois Press, 1975.

Rooney, Jones. *Bossmen: Bill Monroe and Muddy Waters*. New York: Dial Press, 1971.

Russell, Tony. *Blacks, Whites and Blues*. New York: Stein & Day, 1970.

Regional Traditions

We know from recordings that distinctly different blues sounds developed in Texas, Mississippi, Louisiana, Alabama, Georgia, and the Carolinas, but little work has been done on blues as a regional expression. Careful field work is needed to locate singers and trace the history of blues traditions in each area.

Bastin, Bruce. *Crying for the Carolinas*. London: Studio Vista, 1971.

Broven, John. *Walking to New Orleans: The Story of New Orleans Rhythm and Blues*. Bexhill-on-Sea, Sussex, England: Blues Unlimited, 1974.

Ferris, William. *Blues from the Delta*. London: Studio Vista, 1970.

Leadbitter, Mike. *Delta County Blues*. Bexhill-On-Sea: Blues Unlimited, 1968.

Olsson, Bengt. *Memphis Blues*. London: Studio Vista, 1970.

Chicago

Chicago symbolizes the best in urban blues. Musicians migrated to the city from the Deep South and developed a distinct sound which is carefully presented by Charles Keil and Mike Rowe.

Keil, Charles. *Urban Blues*. Chicago: University of Chicago Press, 1967.

Rowe, Mike. *Chicago Breakdown*. London: Eddison Press, 1973.

Blues, Soul, and Rock

Numerous recent studies on soul and rock music show how each is influenced by the blues. As younger performers develop, they reshape the style and verses of blues within their own performances.

Christian, Robert. *Any Old Way You Choose It: Rock and Other Pop Music, 1967–1973*. Baltimore: Penguin Books, 1973.

Cohn, Nik. *Rock*. New York: Pocket Books, 1970.

Garland, Phyl. *The Sound of Soul.* New York: Pocket Books, 1971.

Gillett, Charlie. *The Sound of the City: The Rise of Rock and Roll.* New York: Duterbridge & Dienstfrey, 1970.

Guralnick, Peter. *Feel Like Going Home.* New York: Duterbridge & Dienstfrey, 1971.

Haralambos, Michael. *Right On: From Blues to Soul in Black America.* London: Eddison Press, 1974.

Morse, David. *Grandfather Rock.* New York: Delacorte Press, 1972.

———. *Motown.* New York: Collier Brooks, 1972.

Nicholas, A. X. *The Poetry of Soul.* New York: Bantam Books, 1971.

Shaw, Arnold. *The World of Soul.* New York: Paperback Library, 1971.

Whitcomb, Ian. *After the Ball: Pop Music from Rag to Rock.* Baltimore: Penguin Books, 1974.

Williams, Paul. *Dalton Blues: A Book of Rock Music.* New York: E. P. Dutton, 1969.

Blues Surveys

The work of Paul Oliver is by far the most extensive study of blues by a single person. The following studies by Oliver offer both a comprehensive history of singers and close analysis of their music.

Cook, Bruce. *Listen to the Blues.* New York: Charles Scribner's Sons, 1973.

Murray, Albert. *Stomping the Blues.* New York: McGraw-Hill, 1976.

Oakley, Giles. *The Devil's Music: A History of the Blues.* London: British Broadcasting Corporation, 1976.

Oliver, Paul. *The Meaning of the Blues.* New York: Collier Books, 1966.

———. *Screening the Blues.* London: Cassell, 1968.

———. *The Story of the Blues.* New York: Chilton Book Co., 1969.

Titon, Jeff. *Early Downhome Blues: A Musical and Cultural Analysis.* Urbana, Ill.: University of Illinois Press, 1977.

Records

Our earliest examples of blues are preserved on commercial recordings which date from the 1920s. Carefully developed discographies list title, date, and place of recording for every blues release during the period 1902–66. The history of these recordings is nicely developed in *Recording the Blues.*

Dixon, Robert M. W., and John Godrich. *Blues & Gospel Records: 1902–1942.* London: Storyville Publications, 1969.

———. *Recording the Blues.* New York: Stein & Day, 1970.

Kendziora, Carl Jr. "Perfect Dance and Rock Catalogue," *Record Research*, Issue 51–52, May–June 1963.

Leadbitter, Mike and Neil Slaven. *Blue Records: January, 1943 to December, 1966.* London: Hanover Books, 1968.

Maloney, Don. *The Columbia 13/1400 D Series.* Stanhope, N.J.: Walter C. Allen, 1966.

Vreede, Max E. *Paramount 12000/13000 Series.* London: Storyville, 1971.

How to Play

Books which teach blues guitar, harp, and piano include important introductions and photographs of traditional singers.

Garwood, Donald. *Blues Guitar.* New York: Oak Publications, 1968.

Glover, Tony "Little Son." *Blues Harp.* New York: Oak Publications, 1972.

Grossman, Stefan. *Delta Blues Guitar.* New York: Oak Publications, 1969.

———, Hal Grossman, and Stephen Colt. *Country Blues Songbooks.* New York: Oak Publications, 1973.

Kriss, Eric. *Six Blues-Roots Pianists.* New York: Oak Publications, 1973.

Mann, Woody. *Six Black Blues Guitarists.* New York: Oak Publications, 1973.

Book-Record Studies

Authors of some blues studies have edited records to accompany their work. The following present both the text and sound of blues.

Dixon, Robert, and John Godrich. *Recording the Blues.* New York: Stein & Day, 1970./*Recording the Blues* (CBS 52797).

Evans, David. *Tommy Johnson.* London: Studio Vista, 1971./*The Legacy of Tommy Johnson* (Matchbox SDM 224).

Ferris, William. *Blues from the Delta.* London: Studio Vista, 1970./*Blues from the Delta* (Matchbox SDN 226).

Jackson, Bruce. *Wake Up Dead Man* (Afro-American Work Songs). Cambridge: Harvard University Press, 1972./*Wake Up Dead Man* (Rounder 2018).

Oliver, Paul. *Conversation with the Blues.* New York: Horizon Press, 1965./*Conversation with the Blues* (Decca LK 4664).

———. *Savannah Syncopators.* New York: Stein & Day, 1970./*Sav_ Syncopators* (CBS 52799).

———. *Screening the Blues.* London: Cassell, 1968./*Screening t* (CBS 63288).

———. *The Story of the Blues*. New York: Chilton, 1969./*The Story of the Blues* (Columbia G 30008).

Ramsey, Frederick J. *Been Here and Gone*. New Brunswick: Rutgers University Press, 1960./*Been Here and Gone* (Folkways FA 2659).

Russell, Tony. *Blacks, Whites and Blues*. New York: Stein & Day, 1970./*Blacks, Whites and Blues* (CBS 52796).

Stewart-Baxter, Derrick. *Ma Rainey and the Classic Blues Singers*. New York: Stein & Day, 1970./*Ma Rainey and the Classic Blues Singers* (CBS 52798).

Discography

I Field Recordings

(Listed by Collector)

David Evans

Sorrow Come Pass Me Around (black religious music from Georgia, Louisiana, and Mississippi). Advent 2805.

The Legacy of Tommy Johnson (nine musicians play blues composed by Tommy Johnson). Matchbox SDM 224.

It Must Have Been the Devil (Jack Owens and Bud Spires). Testament T2222.

High Water Blues (Fiddlin' Joe Martin, Woodrow Adams, and Houston Stackhouse). Flyright LP 512.

South Mississippi Blues (bluesmen in the Tylertown area). Rounder Records 2009.

Going up the Country (musicians from Bentonia, Crystal Springs, and Tylertown). Decca LK 4931, Rounder 2012.

Traveling Through the Jungle: Negro Fife and Drum Band Music from the Deep South (fife and drum performers in north Mississippi). Testament T2223.

Roosevelt Holts and His Friends. Arhoolie 1057.

Presenting the Country Blues. Blues Horizon 7–63201.

William Ferris

The Blues Are Alive and Well (performances by James "Son" Thomas, Lee Kizart, and Lovey Williams). Transatlantic Records XTRA 1105. Out of print (hereafter o.p.).

Blues from the Delta (performances by James "Son" Thomas, Lovey Williams, Lee Kizart, and Scott Dunbar). Matchbox SDM 226.

Mississippi Folk Voices (Parchman prison work chants and blues by James "Son" Thomas). Southern Folklore Record 001.

Alan Lomax

Deep South—Sacred & Sinful (blues and gospel recordings—many of which are from Mississippi). Prestige 25005 o.p.

Blues in the Mississippi Night (conversations and music by three Delta bluesmen). United Artists UAL 4027, Vogue VJD 515.

Yazoo Delta Blues and Spirituals. Prestige 25010 o.p.

Negro Prison Songs from the Mississippi State Penitentiary (recorded in 1947 at Parchman Penitentiary). Tradition TLP 1020.

Negro Church Music. Atlantic 1351.

Roots of the Blues (blues and a work chant from Parchman). Atlantic SD 1348 o.p.

Sounds of the South. Atlantic 1346.

Afro-American Spirituals, Work Songs and Ballads. Library of Congress AAFS L3.

Afro-American Blues and Game Songs. Library of Congress AAFS L4. (Both Library of Congress issues are important early recordings with notes made by the Lomaxes during the 1930s and early 1940s.)

The Blues Roll On (Fred McDowell, John Dudley, Rosalie Hill, and non-Mississippi artists). Atlantic 1352 o.p.

John Lomax

Mississippi River Blues. Flyright-Matchbox Library of Congress Series: Vol. 1 50M 230. (Fourteen selections recorded in Natchez on Saturday, October 19, 1940.)

George Mitchell

Mississippi Delta Blues, vols. 1, 2 (recordings made in the late 1960s). Arhoolie 1041, 1042.

Frederick J. Ramsey, Jr.

Been Here and Gone (includes a performance by Scott Dunbar in the early 1950s). Folkways FA 2659.

Chris Strachwitz

I Have to Paint My Face (seven blues performers, including a "talking straight razor" played by Wade Walton). Arhoolie F 1005.

II Anthologies

Adelphi 1005 *Really Chicago Blues* (includes Johnny Shines, Honey Boy Edwards, Walter Horton, and others).

Argo LP 4031 *Folk Festival of the Blues* (1963, Muddy Waters, Sonny Boy Williamson, Howlin' Wolf) o.p.

Aspl. Furry Lewis & Bukka White: *At Home with Friends.*

Blue Thumb 6000 *Memphis Swamp Jam* (1969 recording with selections by Bukka White, Fred McDowell, Napoleon Strickland, and Furry Lewis) o.p.

Blues Classics BC-15 *Memphis and the Delta—'The 1950s.'*

Chess 411 *Drop Down Mama* ('40s and '50s selections by Mississippi-born artists such as Robert Nighthawk, Big Boy Spires, and David Edwards).

Chess (UK) 6641.047, 6641.125, 6641.174 *Genesis* vols. 1, 2, 3 (three four-album boxed sets featuring recordings from '40s and '50s. Mississippi-born artists include Muddy Waters, Sonny Boy Williamson, Robert Nighthawk, Big Bill Broonzy, Sunnyland Slim, and many others).

Decca 4748 *Blues, Southside Chicago* (1965 recordings by Shakey Horton, Johnny Young, Sunnyland Slim, and Robert Nighthawk).

Flyright-Matchbox 230 *Mississippi River Blues* (1940 Library of Congress recordings in Natchez by Lucious Curtis, Willie Ford, and George Baldwin).

Herwin 201 *Sic Em Dogs on Me* (Bukka White, Ishman Bracey, John Hurt, Furry Lewis, and Charley Patton).

Historical Records 22 *They Sang the Blues* (features Robert Wilkins, Skip James, and Furry Lewis).

Kent KST 9009 *Anthology of the Blues: Mississippi Blues* (recordings by Boyd Gilmore, Houton Boines, and Charley Booker in Clarksdale, 1952).

Library of Congress AAFS L59 *Negro Blues and Hollers* (includes two blues by Son House recorded in 1942 by Alan Lomax, Lewis Jones, and John W. Work, and edited by Marshall W. Stearns).

Mamlish S-3802 *Mississippi Bottom Blues* (1926–1935).

Milestone 2016 *The Blues Tradition* (including recordings by Big Bill Broonzy, William Brown, Bobby Grant, and others).

Nighthawk 101 *Windy City Blues* ('30s–'50s Chicago recordings by Mississippi singers such as Robert Lee McCoy and Robert Lockwood).

Origin OJL-5 *The Mississippi Blues*.

Origin OJL-11 *The Mississippi Blues* (vol. 2).

Origin OJL-17 *The Mississippi Blues* (vol. 3) (a three-record set of commercial recordings from the 1920s and 1930s).

Polydor 2383200 *Elmore Jones/Walter Horton* o.p.

PWB2 *Memphis . . . On Down* ('50s recordings by Walter Horton, Willie Love, Charley Booker, Luther Huff, and Boyd Gilmore).

RBF RF-14 *Blues Roots/Mississippi* (an anthology of reissued commercial records from the 1920s to the 1940s).

RCA (Japanese) RA 5708 *Mississippi Blues in the '40s* (selections by Tommy McLennan and Robert Lockwood).

Roots RL-302 *Mississippi Blues—Vol. 1* (1927–42).

Roots RL-303 *Mississippi Blues—Vol. 2* (1927–40).

Roots RL-314 *Mississippi Blues—Vol. 3* (1928–42). (Each of these records includes reissued commercial recordings. Others in the series which include Mississippi bluesmen are RL-313: *Down South* [Louisiana Mississippi-Alabama-Florida, 1927–41] and RL-319: *Up and Down the Mississippi*.)

Sire 97003 1968 *Memphis Country Blues Festival* (selections by Bukka White, Furry Lewis, Robert Wilkins, and Joe Calicott).

Storyville 670180 *Blues Scene U.S.A., Vol. 4: Mississippi Blues*.

Testament 2209 *The Sound of the Delta* (1963–65 recordings of Mississippi bluesmen living in St. Louis).

Vanguard USD 77/78 *Great Bluesmen at Newport* (1959–65 recordings of John Lee Hooker, Son House, John Hurt, Skip James, and Fred McDowell).

Verve FTS-3101 *Living Legends: Son House, Skip James, Bukka White, Big Joe Williams* o.p.

Verve-Forecast VF-9035 *Son House and J. D. Short: Blues from the Mississippi Delta* (House's performances were originally recorded for the Library of Congress in 1942, and Short was rediscovered by Samuel Charters in 1960) o.p.

Yazoo L-1001 *Mississippi Blues 1927–1941.*

Yazoo L-1007 *Jackson Blues 1928–1938.*

Yazoo L-1038 *Lonesome Road Blues: Fifteen Years in the Mississippi Delta 1926–1941.*

Yazoo L-1009 *Mississippi Moaners 1927–1942.* (All of the Yazoo anthologies are reissued commercial recordings with several items issued by the Library of Congress in 1942.)

III Individual Artists

The Aces
The Aces. Vogue (French) LDM 30.174.
Chicago Beat. Black and Blue 33.508.

Bell, Carey
Carey Bell's Blues Harp. Delmark 622.
Last Night. Bluesway 6079 o.p.

Bracey, Ishman
The Famous Tommy Johnson—Ishman Bracey Session. Roots RL 330.

Brewer, Jim
Jim Brewer. Philo 1003.

Broonzy, Big Bill
Big Bill Broonzy. Archive of Folk FS 213.
Big Bill Broonzy. Trip 75000.
Big Bill Broonzy. RCA (French) 7275.
Big Bill Broonzy. Biograph C15.
Big Bill Broonzy. Everest Records FS 213.
Big Bill Broonzy: The Blues. Scepter S-529 o.p.
Big Bill Broonzy. Emarcy LMPG 36137 o.p.
Big Bill Broonzy. Storyville 143.
Big Bill Broonzy Sings Folk Songs. Folkways 2328.
Big Bill Broonzy Sings Country Blues. Folkways 2326.
An Evening wtih Big Bill. Storyville (Danish) SLP 114.
Remembering Big Bill. Mercury SR 60905 o.p.
Make My Getaway. Black and Blue (French) 33.012.
Big Bill Broonzy Memorial. Mercury SR 60822 o.p.
Studs Terkel's Weekly Almanac on Folk Music Blues on WFMT with Big Bill Broonzy and Pete Seeger. Folkways FS 3864.
Big Bill's Blues—Big Bill Broonzy. Columbia LP WL 111 o.p.
Do That Guitar Rag. Yazoo 1035.
An Evenin' with Big Bill. Storyville 143.
Feelin' Low Down. GNP 10004.
Blues with Big Bill Broonzy, Sonny Terry, Brownie McGhee. Folkways FS 3718.
The Big Bill Broonzy Story. Verve MGV 3000-5 o.p.
Big Bill Broonzy Interviewed by Studs Terkel. Folkways FG 3586.
Song and Story. Folkways 3586.

Portraits in Blues, Vol. 1. Storyville 154.
Big Bill Broonzy with Washboard Sam. Chess 1468 o.p.
Big Bill Broonzy Sings Country Blues. Disc. D-112 o.p.
Big Bill Broonzy, Big Bill's Blues. Epic EE 22017 o.p.
The Young Bill Broonzy. Yazoo L-1011.
Big Bill Broonzy Sings Country Blues. Folkways 31005.
Big Bill Broonzy. Storyville 114.
Burn, Eddie
Bottle Up and Go. Action 100.
Callicott, Mississippi Joe
Deal Gone Down. Revival 1002.
Presenting the Country Blues. Blue Horizon 7-63227, o.p. BM & 606.
Carter, Bo
Twist-It Babe. Yazoo 1034.
Bo Carter—Greatest Hits 1930–1940. Yazoo L-1014.
Cat Iron
Blues and Hymns. Folkways FA 2389, XTRA 1087.
Chatmon, Sam
The Mississippi Sheik. Blue Goose 2006.
The New Mississippi Sheiks. Rounder Records 2004.
Collins, Sam
Crying Sam Collins and His Git Fiddle. Origin Jazz Label 10.
Cooke, Sam
Sam Cooke's Best. RCA Victor 2625, 3373.
At the Copa. RCA Victor 2790.
Good News. RCA Victor 2899.
Hits of '50s. RCA Victor 2236.
Mr. Soul. RCA Victor 2673.
Night Beat. RCA Victor 2709.
Shake. RCA Victor 3367.
Try a Little Love. RCA Victor 3435.
Twistin Night Away. RCA Victor 2555.
Unforgettable. RCA Victor 3517.
Cotton, James
100% Cotton. Buddah 5610.
Cut You Loose. Vanguard VSD 79283.
Taking Care of Business. Capitol S7814.
Crudup, Arthur "Big Boy"
Arthur "Big Boy" Crudup. RCA (French) 13Q284 o.p.
Harpin On It. Carnival Juke Blues 5 (only 2 cuts).
The Father of Rock and Roll. RCA LPV 573 o.p.
Look on Yonder's Wall. Delmark DS614.
Roebuck Man. UAS 29092.
Crudup's Mood. Delmark 621.
Mean Ol' Frisco. Fire 1036 (o.p.), Trip 7501.
Davis, Jimmy
Maxwell Street Jimmy Davis. Elektra EKL 303.

Davis, Walter
    Walter Davis & Peetie Wheatstraw: "Down with the Game" 204.
    Think You Need a Shot. RCA INT 1085.
    Walter Davis & Cripple Clarence Lofton. Yazoo 1025.
Diddley, Bo (E. McDaniel)
    Bo Diddley. Checker 1431.
    Bo Diddley in the Spotlight. Checker 2976.
    Go Bo Diddley. Checker 1438.
    Bo Diddley and Company. Checker 2975.
    Beach Party. Checker 2988.
    Bo Diddley. Checker 2984.
    500% More Man. Checker 2996.
    Hey, Good Lookin'. Checker 2992.
    Bo Diddley Is a Gunslinger. Checker 2977.
    Bo Diddley Is a Lover. Checker 2980.
    Bo Diddley Is a Twister. Checker 2982.
    Surfin'. Checker 2987 or Marble Arch (UK) MAL 751
    Another Dimension. Chess 50001/Phonogram (UK) 6310.107.
    Hey, Bo Diddley. Marble Arch (UK) 814 o.p.
    2 Great Guitars. Checker 2991.
    The Super Super Blues Band. Checker 3010/(Chess UK) CRL4529 o.p.
Douglas, K. C.
    K. C. Douglas: Big Road Blues. Bluesville BV 1050.
    K. C.'s Blues. Bluesville 1023.
    K. C. Douglas: A Dead-Beat Guitar and the Mississippi Blues. Cook LP
    5002.
Dunbar, Scott
    Scott Dunbar: From Lake Mary. Ahura Mazda AMSSDS1.
    Blues from the Delta. Matchbox SDM 226.
Fuller, Johnny
    Fuller's Blues. Bluesmaker 3801.
Griffith, Shirley
    The Mississippi Blues. Blue Goose 2011.
    The Blues of Shirley Griffith. Bluesville 1087 o.p.
    Indiana Ave. Blues (with J. T. Adams). Bluesville 1077.
Guitar, Slim
    Guitar Slim—The Things I Used to Do. Specialty SPS 2120.
Holts, Roosevelt
    Roosevelt Holts and His Friends. Arhoolie 1057.
    Presenting the Country Blues. Blue Horizon 7-63201.
Hooker, John Lee
    Moanin' & Stompin' Blues. King 1085 o.p.
    Burnin'. Vee Jay SR 1043 o.p./Joy (UK) 124.
    Concert at Newport. Vee Jay VJS 1078 o.p.
    On Campus. Vee Jay 1066 o.p.
    Endless Boogie. ABC 720.
    Real Blues. Tradition 2089.

I'm John Lee Hooker. Joy (UK) 101.
Never Get Out of These Blues Alive. ABC 736.
Whiskey & Wimmen. Trip TLX 9504.
In Person. VJ Dynasty DY 7301.
John Lee Hooker. Exodus Records EX 325 o.p.
Simply the Truth. Bluesway 6023 o.p.
That's Where It's At. Stax 2013 o.p.
Original Folk Blues. Kent 525.
Big Band Blues. Buddah 7506.
Driftin' Thru the Blues. United 7710.
I Feel Good! Jewell LPS 5005.
The Big Soul. Vee Jay 1058 o.p.
John Lee Hooker and Seven Nights. Verve FT/FTS 3003 o.p.
The Blues. Crown Records CLP 5157 o.p./Kent 559.
House of the Blues. Chess LP 1438 o.p.
At Cafe Au Go Go. Blues 6002 o.p.
Blues Man. Battle 6113 o.p.
Coast to Coast Blues Band. UA 5512 o.p.
No Friend Around. Red Lightin' 003.
Goin' Down Highway 51. Specialty 2127.
Folk Blues. Crown 5295 o.p./United 7729.
Sings the Blues. Crown 5232 o.p.
Slim's Stomp. Polydov 2310256 o.p.
The Great John Lee Hooker. Crown 5333 o.p.
Detroit Special. Atlantic 7228 o.p.
Sings Blues. Ember 3356 o.p.
Live at Sugar Hill. Galaxy 8205.
Cornerstone Collection. Greene Bottle 3130 o.p.
Don't Turn Me from Your Door. Atco 33151, London (UK) 8097 o.p.
How Long Blues. Battle 6114 o.p.
That's My Story/John Lee Hooker Sings the Blues. Riverside 12–321 o.p.
The Folklore of John Lee Hooker. Vee Jay LP 1033 o.p.
John Lee Hooker Sings Blues. King 727 o.p.
The Country Blues of John Lee Hooker. Riverside 12-838 o.p.
John Lee Hooker—Travelin'. Vee Jay LP 1023 o.p.
It Serves You Right. Impulse 9130 o.p.
John Lee Hooker & Big Maceo. Fortune 3002 o.p.
Boogie Chillon. Fantasy 29706.
I Feel Good. Jewel 5005.
John Lee Hooker Plans and Sings the Blues. Chess 1454, Chess (UK) CR1. 4500 o.p.
John Lee Hooker. Everest FS 222.
Urban Blues. Blues Way BLS 6012 o.p.
John Lee Hooker & His Guitar. Advent 2801 o.p.
Vintage Recordings, 1948–52 (three albums). UA LA 127J3 o.p.
Alone. Specialty 2125.
John Lee Hooker. Galaxy 201 o.p.

Horton, Big Walter
  Walter 'Shakey' Horton. Xtra 1135.
  Walter Horton & Floyd Jones. Magnolia 301.
  Big Walter Horton with Carey Bell. Alligator 9702.
  King of the Harmonica Players. Delta 1000.
  An Offer You Can't Refuse. Red Lightnin' 008.
House, Son
  The Legendary 1941, 1942 Recordings. Folk Lyric 9007/Roots RSG-1
  Blind Lemon Jefferson/Son House. Biograph BLP 12040.
  Blues from the Mississippi Delta: Son House and J. D. Short. Verve
    FV9035 o.p.
  Father. Columbia CS 9217, CL2417.
  The Real Delta Blues. Blue Goose 2016.
  Blues from the Mississippi Delta. Verve/Fore 9035 o.p.
  Mississippi Delta. Folkways 2467.
  Son House & Robert Pete Williams Live. Roots 501.
  Living Legends. Verve FT 3010 o.p.
  Son House and J. D. Short—Delta Blues. Folkways FTS 31028/XTRA
    (UK) 1080.
  The Vocal Intensity of Son House. Roots SL 504.
Howlin' Wolf (Chester Burnett)
  London Revisited. Chess 60026 (with Muddy Waters).
  Howlin' Wolf. Chess 1469.
  Moanin' in the Moonlight. Chess 1434 o.p./Chess 1540.
  Back Door Wolf. Chess 50045.
  The London Howlin' Wolf Sessions. Chess 60008.
  The Best of Howlin' Wolf. Chess (Japan) 6130.
  More Real Folk Blues. Chess 1512 o.p.
  Message to the Young. Phonogram (UK) 6310 108.
  The Real Folk Blues. Chess 1502 o.p.
  The Super Super Blues Band. Checker 3010 o.p.
  *This Is Howlin' Wolf's New Album. He doesn't Like It. He Didn't Like
    His Electric Guitar at First Either.* Cadet LPS 319. o.p.
  Howlin' Wolf—Big City Blues. United Records UM 717/Crown 5240.
  Evil. Chess 1540.
  Original Folk Blues. Kent 526.
  Live and Cookin' at Alice's Revisited. Chess CH 50015.
  Going Back Home. Syndicate Chapter SC003.
  Change My Way. Chess 418.
  A Howlin' Wolf. Chess 2ACMB 201/Chess 60016.
Hurt, Mississippi John
  Mississippi John Hurt. Vanguard 9220.
  Mississippi John Hurt, Folk Songs and Blues. Piedmont 13157.
  Worried Blues. Piedmont 13161
  The Immortal Mississippi John Hurt. Vanguard VSD 79248.
  Last Sessions. Vanguard VSD 79327.
  The Best of Mississippi John Hurt. Vanguard VSD 19/20.

Mississippi John Hurt—The Original 1928 Recordings. Spokane SPL 1001 o.p.

Mississippi John Hurt: His First Recordings. Biograph BLP C4.

Volume One of a Legacy. Rebel 1068.

James, Elmore

Elmore James. Bell 6037 o.p.

The Great Elmore James. Up Front 122.

Tough (with John Brim). Blue Horizon 763204 o.p.

Something Inside of Me. Bell MBLL 104 (U.K.) o.p.

Whose Muddy Shoes (with John Brim). Chess 1537.

To Know a Man. Blue Horizon 7-66230 o.p.

Blues After Hours. Crown 5168 o.p.

Elmore James & Eddie Taylor. Cobblestone 9001/Muse 5087.

Elmore James. Blue Horizon BM4601 o.p.

Elmore James. BYG 529004 o.p.

Legend of Elmore James. UAS 29109 (U.K.) o.p.

The Best of Elmore James. Sue Records ILP 918 o.p.

Original Folk Blues—Elmore James. Kent KLP 522.

The Legend of Elmore James. Kent KST 9001/United 7778.

The Resurrection of Elmore James. Kent KST 9010/United 7787.

History of Elmore James. Trip TLX 9511.

Blues in My Heart, Rhythm in My Soul. United 7716.

Elmore James Memorial Album. Sue Records ILP 927 o.p.

I Need You. Sphere Sound 7008 o.p.

James, Skip

King of the Delta Blues Singers. Biography 12029.

Skip James, Greatest of the Delta Blues Singers. Melodeon 7321.

Today! Vanguard 79219.

Living Legends. Verve RT 3010 o.p.

Devil Got My Woman. Vanguard VSD 79273.

A Tribute to Skip James. Biograph 12016.

Johnson, Robert

Robert Johnson. Kokomo 1000 o.p.

Robert Johnson, King of the Delta Blues Singers. Columbia CL 1654.

King of the Delta Blues Singers: Volume II. Columbia C3003/CBS (UK) 64102.

Delta Blues (also Patton, House, James). Roots 339.

Johnson, Tommy

The Famous Tommy Johnson-Ishman Bracey Session. Roots RL330.

King, Albert

Truckload of Lovin'. Utopia 1–1387.

Wanna Get Funny. Star 5585.

Jammed Together. Stax 2020 o.p.

Live Wire. Stax 2003 o.p.

Lovejoy. Stax 2040 o.p.

Years Gone By. Stax 2010 o.p.

King of the Blues Guitar. Atlantic SD 8213.

King Does the King's Things. Stax ST 2015 o.p.
Born Under a Bad Sign. Stax S723 o.p.
I'll Play the Blues for You. Stax STS3009 o.p.
Door to Door (one side of album by Otis Rush). Chess 1538.
Travelin' to California. Starday King Records, KSD 1060.
Live. Utopia CYL2-2205.

King, B. B.
Blues for Me. United 7708.
Lucille. Bluesway BLS 6016 o.p.
Mr. Blues. ABC 456.
Blues Is King. Blues 6001.
Blues on Top of Blues. Blues 6011.
Confessin' the Blues. ABC 528.
Live at the Regal. ABC 509/ABC 724.
Live & Well. Bluesway BLS 6031/ABC 819.
Completely Well. BLS 6037/ABC 868/Probe (UK) SSL 10299.
Indianola Mississippi Seeds. ABCS-713/Probe (UK) SPBA 6255.
Greatest Hits. Galaxy 8208.
His Best. Bluesway 6022.
Torn onto B. B. King. Stateside (UK) SCO54-90296.
Blues Is King. ABC 704.
King Size. ABC 977.
To Know You Is to Love You. ABC Records ABCX 794.
Don't Answer the Door. Bluesway BLS 6001.
In London. ABC 730/Probe (UK) SPB 1041.
The Best of B. B. King. ABC 767.
The Electric B. B. King—His Best. ABC 794.
Back in the Alley. ABC 878.
Guess Who. ABC Records ABCX 759.
Sweet Sixteen. Kent 568.
B. B. King Live. Kent KST 565X/United 7736.
Doing My Thing Lord. Kent 563.
Take a Swing with Me. Polydor (UK) 2431.004.
B. B. King on Stage. Kent KST 515.
The Incredible Soul of B. B. King. Kent KST 539.
B. B. King—L. A. Midnight. ABC Records ABCX 743.
Lucille Talks Back. ABC 898.
From the Beginning. Kent KST 533.
Live in Cook County Jail. ABC Records ABCS 723/Probe (UK) SPB1032.
B. B. King-Friends. ABC Records ABCD 825.
B. B. King 1949–1950. Kent KST 9011.
The Jungle. Kent KST 521.
B. B. King Better Than Ever. Kent KST 561.
Rock Me Baby. Kent KST 512/United 7733.
Easy Listening Blues. United Records 7705.
Let Me Love You. Kent KST 513/United 7734.

Boss of the Blues: B. B. King. Kent KST 529.
Heart Full of Blues. United 7703.
King of the Blues. United 7730.
I Love You So. United 7711.
Singing the Blues. United 7726.
Great B. B. King. United 7728.
The Soul of B. B. King. United 7714.
The Blues. United 7732.
King, Little Freddy
Harmonica Williams with Freddy King. Ahura Mazda AMS 2003.
Lenoir, J. B.
Alabama Blues. CBS 62593 o.p.
Natural Man. Chess 410.
J. B. Lenoir. Polydor 244011 o.p./Polydor (UK) 2482014 o.p.
J. B. Lenoir, Python 25.
Lewis, Furry
Shake Em On Down. Fantasy 24703.
Fourth and Beale. Barclay 80.602.
In His Prime, 1927–29. Yazoo 1050.
Live at the Gaslight. Ampex 10140.
In Memphis. Matchbox 190/Roots 505.
The Early Years, 1927–29. Spokane 1009 o.p.
Done Changed My Mind. Bluesville 1037 o.p.
Back on My Feet Again. Bluesville 1036 o.p.
Furry Lewis. Folkways FS 3823/XTRA (UK) 1116.
Little Milton (Milton Campbell)
Greatest Hits. Chess 50013.
Waiting for Little Milton. Stax 3012.
Raise a Little Sand. Red Lightnin' 0011.
Little Milton. Chess 2ACMB 204.
Friend of Mine. Glades 7508.
If Walls Could Talk. Checker LPS 3012 o.p.
Grits Ain't Groceries. Checker LPS 3011 o.p.
We're Gonner Make It. Checker 2995 o.p.
Littlejohn, John
Funky from Chicago. Bluesway 6069 o.p.
John Littlejohn's Chicago Blues Stars. Arhoolie 1043.
McClennan, Tommy
Tommy McClennan. Roots 305.
Highway 51. Flyright 112.
Tommy McClennan. RCA (French) 130.274 o.p.
McDowell, Fred
Mississippi Fred McDowell, 1904–1972. Sunshine.
Just Sunshine. J554/XTRA 1136.
Long Way from Home. Milestone 3004.
In London. Sive 97018 o.p.
Amazing Grace. Testament 2219.

8 Years Rambling! Revival 1001 o.p./Rounder 2007.
Fred McDowell & His Blues Boys. Arhoolie 1046.
Keep Your Lamp Trimmed. Arhoolie 1068.
Live in New York. Oblivion 001.
In London, Vols. 1 & 2. TRA 194.203.
Going Down South, Polydor 236.570.
Somebody Keeps Callin' Me. Antilles 7022.
Mississippi Fred McDowell. Everest FS253.
My Home Is in the Delta. Testament T 2208.
Mississippi Delta Blues. Arhoolie F1021.
Fred McDowell: I Do Not Play No Rock and Roll. Capital ST 409.
Mississippi Delta Blues. Polydor 2460.193.
Fred McDowell. Arhoolie F1027.

Macon, Shortstuff
Hell Bound & Heaven Sent. Folkways 3100.
Mr. Shortstuff. Spivey 1005.

Magic Sam (Samuel Maghett)
West Side Soul—Magic Sam's Blues Band. Delmark DS 615.
Black Magic. Delmark 620.
1937–1969. Blue Horizon 763223 o.p.

Mississippi Sheiks
Stop & Listen. Mamlish 3809.

Nighthawk, Robert
Robert Nighthawk-Houston Stackhouse. Testament T 2215.
Drop Down Mama. Chess 411 (includes other artists).

Patton, Charley
The Immortal Charley Patton. Origin Jazz Label 1.
The Immortal Charley Patton. Origin Jazz Label 2.
Charley Patton: Founder of the Delta Blues. Yazoo L1020.

Pryor, Snooky
——— *and the Country Blues.* Today 1012 o.p.
Snooky Prior. Flyright 100.
Do It If You Want To. Bluesway 6076 o.p.

Reed, Jimmy
The Bossman of the Blues. VJ 1080 o.p.
The Best of the Blues. VJ 1072 o.p.
As Jimmy Is. Roker 4001 o.p.
Blues Is My Business. VJ 7303.
Let the Bossman Speak. Blues on Blues 1001 o.p.
The New Jimmy Reed Album. Blues Way (ABC Records) BL 6004 o.p.
Jimmy Reed: Found Love. Vee Jay 1022 o.p.
Soulin. Bluesway 6009 o.p.
Down in Virginia. Bluesway 6034.
Down in Virginia. Vee Jay 287 o.p.
Jimmy Reed at Carnegie Hall. Vee Jay 1035 o.p.
I Ain't from Chicago. Bluesway 6054.
Jimmy Reed at Carnegie Hall. Vee Jay 1035 o.p.

The Very Best of Jimmy Reed. Buddah Records BDS 4003 o.p.
Wailin' the Blues. Tradition 2069.
Roots of the Blues. Kent 537.
The Ultimate Jimmy Reed. Bluesway 6067 o.p.
Greatest Hits. Kent 553.
The History of Jimmy Reed. Trip 8012.
The History of Jimmy Reed, Vol. 2. Trip 9515.
Big Bossman. Bluesway 6015 o.p.
Jimmy Reed. Archive of Folk 234.

Robinson, Fenton
  Somebody Loan Me a Dime. Alligator 4705.

Rogers, Jimmy
  Blues All Day Long. Advent LLP 1 o.p.
  Gold Tailed Bird. Shelter 8921 o.p.
  Chicago Bound. Chess 407.

Ross, Isaiah "Doctor"
  The Harmonica Boss. Big Bear 2.
  Doctor Ross—His First Recordings. Arhoolie 1065.
  Call the Doctor. Testament 2206.
  Live at Montreux. Polydor 2460-169 o.p.
  Doctor Ross: The Harmonica Boss. Fortune FS3011 o.p.

Rush, Otis
  Mourning in the Morning. Atlantic 40.495.
  This One's a Good Un. Blue Horizon 763222 o.p.
  Door to Door. Chess 1538.
  Right Place, Wrong Time. Bullfrog 301.
  Blues Live. Trio (Japan) 3086.

Short, J. D.
  J. D. Short. Sonet 648.

Smith, Robert Curtis
  The Blues of Robert Curtis Smith. Bluesville 1064 o.p.

Spann, Otis
  Biggest Thing Since Colossus. Blue Horizon 4802 o.p./Blue Horizon (UK) 763217 o.p.
  Otis Spann Is the Blues. Barnaby 30246 o.p.
  The Blues Never Die. Prestige 7391 o.p./Prestige 7719.
  The Blues Is Where It's At. Bluesway BL 6003 o.p.
  Otis Spann. Everest FS 216/Storyville 157.
  The Bottom of the Blues. Bluesway BLS 6013 o.p.
  Walking the Blues. Barnaby 31290 o.p.
  Cracked Spinner Head. Devam 1036 o.p.
  Otis Spann's Chicago Blues. Testament 2211.
  Heart Loaded with Trouble. Bluesway 6063 o.p.
  Cryin' Time. Vanguard 6514.
  Sweet Giant of the Blues. Bluestime 29006.

Stackhouse, Houston
  Robert Nighthawk-Houston Stackhouse. Testament T-2215.

Stovall, Babe
  Babe Stovall. Verve VPM 1 o.p.
Sunnyland, Slim
  Sunnyland Slim. Sonet 671.
  Depression Blues. Festival (France) FLO 648.
  Slim's Got His Thing Goin' On. World Pacific Records WPS 21890 o.p.
  Midnight Jump. Blue Horizon 7463213 o.p.
  Plays the Ragtime Blues. Bluesway 6068.
  Portrait in Blues—Sunnyland Slim. Storyville SLP 169.
  Chicago Blues Sessions (with Little Brother Montgomery). "77"LA12/21.
  Slim's Shout. Prestige PR7723.
  Sad and Lonesome. Jewel 5010.
Taylor, Eddie
  Eddie Taylor & Floyd Jones. Testament 2214.
  I Feel So Bad. Advent 2802.
  Elmore James & Eddie Taylor. Cobblestone 9001 o.p./Muse 5087.
  Ready for Eddie. Big Bear 2.
Taylor, Hound Dog
  Hound Dog Taylor. Alligator 4701.
  Hound Dog Taylor, Vol. 2. Alligator 4704.
  Beware of the Dog. Alligator 4707.
Townsend, Henry
  Tired of Bein' Mistreated. Bluesville 1041 o.p.
  Music Man. Adelphi 1016.
Turner, Ike
  Ike & Tina Turner's Greatest Hits. Warner Bros. W1810 o.p.
  A Black Man's Soul. Pompeii SD 6003 o.p.
  Cussin', Cryin', & Carryin' On. Pompeii S 96004 o.p.
  River Deep-Mountain High. Phil Spector SP 4178.
  Ike—Tina. Blue Thumb BTS 5. o.p.
  In Person—Ike & Tina Turner. Minit LP 24018 o.p.
  Ike & Tina Turner Revue Live. Kent 515.
Waters, Muddy (McKinley Morganfield)
  The London Muddy Waters Sessions. Chess 60013.
  After the Rain. Cadet LPS 320 o.p.
  Muddy Waters at Newport. Chess 1449/Pye (UK) NJL 34.
  The Songs of Big Bill Broonzy. Chess 1444 o.p.
  Muddy Waters' Best. Chess 1427 o.p./Chess 1539.
  Brass and Blues. Chess 1507.
  Hard Again. Columbia PZ 34449.
  London Revisited. Chess 60026 (with Howlin' Wolf).
  Unk in Funk. Chess 60031.
  Woodstock Album. Chess 60035.
  The London Muddy Waters Sessions. Chess CH 60013.
  "Live." Chess 50012.
  Folk Singer. Chess 1483.
  More Real Folk Blues. Chess 1511 o.p.

Real Folk Blues. Chess 1501/Chess (UK) 4515 o.p.
The Super Super Blues Band. Checker 3010.
Sail On. Chess 1539.
They Call Me Muddy Waters. Chess CH 1553.
Good News. Syndicate Chapter SC 002.
Back in the Early Days (two records). Syndicate Chapter SC 001/2.
Vintage Muddy Waters. Sunnyland KS100.
The Best of Muddy Waters. Chess 1427.
Muddy Sings Delta Blues. Chess (Japan) 6137.
Best of Muddy Waters. Chess (Japan) 8343.
McKinley Morganfield AKA Muddy Waters. Chess 60006.
Can't Get No Grindin'. Chess 50023.
Electric Mud. Cadet Concept LPS 314 o.p.
Down on Stovall's Plantation. Testament T 2210.
White, Bukka
Bukka White. CBS 52629 o.p.
Mississippi Blues. Bukka White. Takoma B-1101/Sonet 609
Baton Rouge, Moseby Street. Blues Beacon 1932.119.
Memphis Hot Shots. Blue Horizon 763229.
Big Daddy. Biograph 12044.
"Sky Songs." Arhoolie F 1019, 1020.
Country Blues. Sparkussp. (German) 1.
Wilkins, Robert
Rev. Robert Wilkins. Piedmont 13162.
Early Recordings. Magpie 1800.
Williams, Big Joe
Hand Me Down My Walking Stick. World Pacific 21897 o.p.
Blues for G Strings. Bluesville 1056 o.p.
Crawlin' Kingsnake. RCS Int 1087 o.p.
Big Joe Williams. Storyville 163/Archive of Folk FS 218.
Big Joe Williams. Storyville 224.
Blues Bash. Olympia 7115.
Big Joe Williams. Sonet 635.
The Blues Box. Verve FTS. (Big Joe is only one of many on this album.)
Piney Woods Blues. Delmark 602.
Thinking of What They Did to Me. Arhoolie 1053.
Back to the Country. Testament 2205.
Blues on Highway 49. Delmark 604.
Crawlin' Kingsnake. RCA (Japanese) RA 5701.
Classic Delta Blues. Milestone 3001.
Stavin' Chain Blues. Delmark 609.
Tough Times. Arhoolie 1002.
Traditional Blues. Folkways 3820.
Big Joe Williams and Short Stuff Macon: Hell Bound and Heaven Sent. Folkways FTS 31004.
Big Joe Williams and Sonny Boy Williamson. Arhoolie Blues Classics 21.
Living Legends. Verve FT 3010 o.p.

Blues from the Mississippi Delta. Blues on Blues 1003 o.p.
Don't Your Peaches Look Mellow. Bluesway 6080 o.p.
Malvina, My Sweet Womun. Oldie Blues 2804.
Williamson, Sonny Boy
  Sonny Boy Williamson & Memphis Slim in Paris. Crescendo 10003.
  The Night Time Is the Right Time. Springboard 4065.
  Rock Generation, Vol. 9. BYB 529.709.
  One Way Out. Chess 417.
  King Biscuit Time. Arhoolie 2020.
  Down & Out Blues. Chess 1437.
  Bummer Road. Chess 1536.
  This Is My Story. Chess 1536.
  In Memorium. Chess (UK) 4510 o.p.
  Sonny Boy Williamson. Storyville 158. *Volume 2.* Storyville 170.
Young, Johnny
  I Can't Keep My Foot from Jumping. Bluesway 6075 o.p.
  Johnny Young & Friends. Testament 2226.
  Chicago Blues. Arhoolie 1037.
  Blues Masters, Vol. 9. Blue Horizon 4609.
  ——*and His Chicago Blues Band.* Arhoolie 1029.

NOTE: Most of these records may be obtained through two distributors
who specialize in blues and other folk recordings:

Muscadine Records
42 North Lake
Pasadena, California 91101.

Rounder Records
186 Willow Avenue
Somerville, Massachusetts 02144

Filmography

The following films are on Mississippi performers. For a complete list of films available on blues see: *American Folklore Films and Videotape: An Index* (Memphis, Tennessee: Center for Southern Folklore, 1976).

Delta Blues Singer: James "Sonny" Thomas: Focuses on the life of blues musician James Thomas. The film records Thomas playing his "bottleneck" style in local jook joints near his home, sculpting unusual skulls, faces, and animals from Delta buckshot clay, and talking about his family and his work.

Give My Poor Heart Ease: Mississippi Delta Bluesmen: A personal account of the blues experience through recollections and performances by B. B. King, inmates from Mississippi's Parchman Prison, musicians in a Leland jook joint, a barber from Clarksdale, and a salesman at a Beale Street clothing store. Musical selections include prison work chants, "Highway 61," "Rock Me, Momma," "Hoochie Koochie Man," and B. B. King's "The Thrill Is Gone."

Gravel Springs Fife and Drum: Focuses on the northwest Mississippi community of Gravel Springs. Othar Turner, leader of a musical group, works on his farm, makes a cane fife, and travels to a rural picnic where he and his band play music for their friends. The unusual fife and drum music they perform closely resembles traditional West African sounds.

I Ain't Lying: Folktales from Mississippi: Captures the humor and drama of black folktales in Leland and Rose Hill, Mississippi. Mary Gordon, Rev. Isaac Thomas, "Poppa Jazz" Brown, and James "Sonny Ford" Thomas tell religious and protest tales that celebrate folk characters such as the preacher and John. Includes Poppa Jazz's version of "Heaven and Hell."

Mississippi Delta Blues: A collection of performances filmed 1968–70. The film begins with Louis Dotson playing his "one-strand on the wall." From Dotson's home the film moves to Shelby "Poppa Jazz" Brown's jook joint in Leland, Mississippi. James "Son" Thomas and "Little Son" Jefferson play while couples dance the boogie and slow drag. Wade Walton uses his barber's razor and leather strap to strike the beat as he performs his original

"Barber Shop Boogie." Walton's friends include blues piano player "Pine Top" Johnson, who plays "Pine Top Boogie Woogie."

[The above films are distributed by the Center for Southern Folklore, 1216 Peabody Avenue, P. O. Box 4081, Memphis, Tennessee, 38104.]

Fred McDowell: Blues Maker: Includes interviews with McDowell and several of his blues. Homes and fields around McDowell's home town of Como are shown.

They Sing of a Heaven: Shows the history of Mississippi Sacred Harp singing with sections on black churches in northeastern Mississippi.

[Both of the above films are distributed by the Department of Film Production, University of Mississippi, University, Mississippi, 38677.]

Accommodation by blacks, associated
  with blues, 45
Africa, 25
Age, and musical preference, 45–46,
  47–48
"Ain't That Loving You Baby," 192,
  193
"All Night Long," 191, 193
Alligator, Miss., 3
Allison, Mose, 96, 190
Anguilla, Miss., 3
Arcola, Miss., 3
Audience participation in blues
  performance, 101, 103, 104–13, 115
  passim

"Baby, Please Don't Go," 61, 71, 189,
  190, 193
Baby Sister, 104, 107, 112, 138, 148, 153,
  155
Berimbau, Afro-Brazilian musical
  instrument, 184
Birdie, Miss., 12, 47
"Black Night," 130, 192
Blacks: blues singers as spokesmen for,
  9, 31; and development of Miss.
  Delta, 3–4; different blues repertoires
  and styles for whites and, 91, 96–97;
  and early record players, 8–9;
  employment, housing of, in Delta, 7,
  13, 15; lynching, massacre of, 18–19,
  191; migration of, 6–7, 111, 179–80;
  population of, in Delta, 7; and "soul"
  music, 45; work songs of, 32
Blind Lemon (Blind Lemon Jefferson),
  9, 46, 189
Blues: bands, 48–49, 51–52; black vs.
  white views of, 91; circulation of, 31,
  36; defined, xi–xii, 25–26; function of,
  48, 53; generational views on, 45–50;
  and hymns, 80–81, 83–84; influences
  on, xi, 9, 31–32, 35, 52–54, 62;
  male-female perspective of, 27; origin,
  development of, xi, 25, 26, 28, 31–32,
  35, 41–43, 48; performed at house
  parties and jook joints, 19–22, 58, 101,
  103–5, 112–13, 115 *passim;* preference
  for, in Delta, 96–97; religious hostility
  to, 82, 83–85; styles of, 36, 37, 39, 47,
  48–49, 51–52, 80; violence at sessions,
  95–96, 101–3. *See also* Verses (blues).
Blues singers: and blues "talk sessions,"
  103, 104–5, 107–12, 115 *passim;* and
  circulation of blues, 31, 36; and
  composition of blues, 57–59, 61–65,
  67–71; generational views of, 46–47,
  48–49; influence of, from Delta, 8, 9;
  influences on, 46–47, 51–52, 53;
  nicknames of, 13; religious hostility
  to, 79, 82–85; repertoires, styles of, 91;
  sense of place of, 28; spokesmen for
  black community, 9, 25, 31, 41; and
  voodoo, 77–78

Bo Diddley (Ellas McDaniel), 9
Boogie (dance), 70, 92
"Bottle 'Em Up and Go," 189, 190, 193
Brazil, 37, 183, 184
Broonzy, William Lee "Big Bill," 31,
  35–36, 188
Brown, James (soul singer), 45, 47, 48,
  53
Brown, Shelby "Poppa Jazz," 6–7, 13,
  15–21, 22–24, 41–42, 64, 65, 85,
  86–89, 159, 160, 161

Cairo, Ill., 23
California, 110, 118, 120, 124, 127
Callion, Ella Mae, 73–74
Charles, Ray, 9, 80
Chicago, Ill.: 81; black migration to,
  6–7, 8, 110, 111; in blues, 28, 29, 122,
  130, 135; records made in, 191, 192,
  193
Chinese, in Miss., 7
Church of God in Christ. *See* Sanctified
  Church.
Cicero, Ill., 8, 130
Civil rights, 3, 17, 45
Clarksdale, Miss., 4, 8, 25, 84, 91, 96,
  101, 103, 109, 110, 112, 118, 120, 124,
  127, 134, 147, 149
Collins, Eddie, 92, 189
Cooper, Joe, 21, 67–70
Cotton, cultivation of, 3, 5, 8
Country music, 92, 96–97, 190
Cox, Ida, 102
Crawford, Miss., 184
Crudup, Arthur "Big Boy," 8, 51–52, 93,
  189, 191

Dahomey, 77, 183
Dallas, Texas, 160
Dances, accompanied by blues, 45–46
Davis, Tyrone, 73
Davis, Walter, 78, 154, 187, 193
Decatur, Ala., 121, 122
Delta (Miss.): 102, 109; and black
  migration, 3, 6; blues singers from, xi,
  8, 9, 180; development, characteristics
  of blues in, xi, 36, 46, 53, 58, 71,
  79–80, 96; economy of, 3–4;
  employment and housing of blacks in,
  7, 15; population of, 7; Sanctified
  Church in, 84–85; settlement of, 3–4;
  soul music in, 46–47; typography and
  soil of, 3, 8
Depression (economic), 111, 129–30
Depression (emotional), 48, 53
Detroit, Mich., 111, 135
Dotson, Louis, 38
"Down by the Riverside," 95, 189
Dozens, 108, 191, 193
Drew, Miss., 57
"Drifting Blues," 105, 192
Dumas, Tom, 96–97
Dunbar, Scott, 95–96, 190

Dupree, Champion Jack, 187, 193
"Dust My Broom," 109, 192

East St. Louis, Ill., 34, 191
Eden, Miss., 22
Escape, theme of, in work songs and
  blues, 32, 35, 110
"Ethel Mae," 52, 189

Fats Domino, 192
Florence, Ala., 8, 184
Folk music, xi, 180
Folklorists, 36, 180
Folklore motifs, defined, 180
"Forty-Four Blues," 71, 189
Franklin, Aretha, 45
Freedmen, migration to Miss. Delta, 3–4
Frost, Frank, 53

Ghettos, 25, 28
Glendora, Miss., 103
"Going Down Slow," 110, 192
Grafton, Wisc., 192
"Grand Ole Opry," 92, 96
Grant and Wilson (Leola B. and Kid
  Wesley Wilson), 182
Greenwood, Miss., 84
Grenada, Miss., 78, 184
Griots, 25, 182
Guitars, 31, 38, 39, 184

Haiti, 183
Handy, William Christopher, 8, 31, 36,
  184
Hawkins, Erskine, 124
Helena, Ark., 182
Herbal root, voodoo and sexual image
  in blues, 77–78
"Hoochie Koochie Man," 107, 153,
  187, 193
"Hook It to the Mule" (dance), 46
Hoover, Herbert, 111, 129
Hopkins, Sam "Lightning," 9
House, Eddie James "Son," Jr., 8
Housing, of blacks in Delta, 7, 15
Houston, Texas, 191, 193
"How Long—How Long Blues," 192,
  193
Howlin' Wolf (Chester Burnett), xi, 8,
  189
Humor, in blues verses, 26
Hymns: 31; blues singers reluctant to
  sing, 81–82; coded messages in, 110,
  122; similarities to blues, 79–80,
  80–81, 83, 84

Indianapolis, Ind., 192
Italians, in Miss., 7

Jackson, Melvin "Little Son," 188, 189,
  191–92
Jackson, Miss., 8, 58, 74, 91, 109, 127,
  192
James, Elmore, 39, 52, 93, 189, 192
James, Skip, 8, 188

Jefferson, "Little Son," 21, 23, 160, 161,
  189
Jim Crow laws, 9, 25
"John Henry," 57, 70
"John the Conqueror Root" (herbal
  root), 77–78, 153
Johnson, Lonnie, 46
Johnson, Robert, 8, 93, 189, 192
Johnson, Tommy, 186, 189
Johnson, Wallace "Pine Top," 13, 26,
  27, 49, 78, 103–5, 107–12, 115–59
Jokes, in blues performance, 101
Jones, Eddie "One String," 184, 193
"Jook," 58, 181
Jordan, Louis, 102, 143, 193
Journal of a Residence on a Georgia
  Plantation in 1838–1839, 31–32

Kemble, Frances Anne, 31–32
King, Riley B. "B.B.," xi, 8, 26, 27, 28,
  37–38, 46, 73, 74–75, 182
Kizart, Lee, 80, 81–82, 84–85, 102–3,
  104, 160, 163

Labor, of blacks, in settling Delta, 3–4;
  theme of, in blues, 25–26, 35, 41–42,
  108; work songs as means of pacing,
  32–33
Lake Mary, Miss., 95, 96
Lambert, Miss., 32
Landowners (white), and
  sharecroppers' indebtedness, 3–6
Las Vegas, Nev., 159
Leland, Miss., 3, 7, 13, 17–19, 22, 46, 91,
  160
Lenoir (Lenore), J. B., 189, 192
Lexington, Miss., 91
"Little Honey Bee," 61–62
"Little Liza Jane," 189, 190
Little Milton (Milton Anderson), 74
"Little Red Shoes," 92, 93, 189
Little Walter (Marion Walter Jacobs),
  52, 191
Loneliness, theme of, in blues and
  religious music, 79–80
Los Angeles, Cal., 191, 192
Louis, Joe "Big Daddy" (disc jockey),
  74–75
Louise, Miss., 8
Louisiana, 120, 148
Love, theme in blues and work songs,
  26–28, 32–33, 35, 42, 48, 61, 108
Love, Jasper, 4, 8, 25–26, 101, 104, 105,
  107, 108–9, 110, 111, 112, 155–56,
  159–60, 164–65, 166–67, 179, 181
Lula, Miss., 3, 53, 80
Lynching, of blacks, 7, 18–19

McGee, Rev. F. W., 57
McGhee, "Brownie" (Walter Brown
  McGhee), 187, 193
Maghett, Samuel "Magic Sam," 184
"Make ups." See Verses (blues).
Matthews, William "Sonny," 57, 80
Memphis, Tenn., 3, 159

Memphis Minnie and Kansas Joe (Minnie and Joe McCoy), 182
Migration of blacks from Miss., 6–7, 111, 179–80
Mississippi (state): 28, 159; black migration from, 6–7, 111, 180; in blues "talk," 105, 109, 110, 118, 120, 131, 133; Chinese, Italians, Syrians in, 7; emotional connotations of, 105, 109, 110. See also Delta (Miss.).
Mississippi River, 3
Mobile, Ala., 109, 127
Montgomery, Eurreal "Little Brother," 189, 192
Moorhead, Miss., 8, 28, 184
Muddy Waters (McKinley Morganfield), xi, 8, 61–62, 78, 109, 153, 187, 189, 191, 193
Music. See Blues; Country music; Folk music; Hymns; Sacred harp singing; Soul music; Spirituals.

Nashville, Tenn., 96, 124
Natchez, Miss., 28
Needle, sexual image of, in blues, 78
New Orleans, La., 152, 192
New York, N.Y., 193
Nitta Yuma, Miss., 3
North, black migration to, 6–7, 111

Obscenity, in blues, 15, 67–70, 91, 108
"Ohio River Bridge," 21–22
"Old Hen Cackle," 189, 190
"One Room Country Shack," 108, 117, 191
One-strand-on-the-wall (musical instrument), 37, 38, 62
O'Neil, Arthur "Poppa Neil," 21
Onward, Miss., 3
Owens, Jack, 188

Pain, theme of, in blues, 41
Panther Burn, Miss., 3
Parchman Prison, Miss., 32–33
Parker, "Little Junior," 93, 188, 191, 193
Patton, Charley, 8, 188
Perkins, Joe Willie "Pine Top," 104
Pickett, Wilson (soul singer), 48
"Pine Top Boogie Woogie," 107–8, 109, 110, 111, 115, 126, 127, 191, 192
Population in Miss. Delta, 7
Port Gibson, Miss., 77
Preachers, hostility to blues, 79, 82–83, 83–84
Presley, Elvis, xi, 189, 193
Protest, theme of, in blues, 12, 15
Proverbs, blues verses' similarity to, 73

Quesie, Eddie, 21, 65

Race: taboos of, in South, 11–12; theme of, in blues, 15, 26, 91
"Race" records, 8, 27, 36
Railroad work songs, 34–35

Rainey, Gertrude "Ma," 27, 193
Reconstruction, 25
Record players, 8–9
Records: and flexibility of blues verses and titles, 70–71; influence on blues, xi, 51–54, 58–59, 62; limitations of, in studying oral tradition, 103. See also "Race" records.
Reed, Jimmy, 9, 192
Religion, influence on blues, 28
"Rock Me, Momma," 189, 191
"Rockin' and Rollin'," 191–92
Rodgers, Jimmie, xi, 183
Rolling Fork, Miss., 185, 188
Rolling Stones, xi
Roosevelt, Franklin D., 130
Rose Hill, Miss., 188
"Rumble Go the Train," 62–64
"Running Wild," 111, 140

Sacred harp singing, 96
St. Louis, Mo., 6, 193
San Antonio, Tex., 192, 193
Sanctified Church, hostility to blues, 84–85
"Santa Fe Blues," 109, 192
Santa Fe Railroad, 127, 128, 129
Sense of place, in blues verses, 28
Sex, theme of, in blues, 26–28, 81
Sexual symbolism in blues, 77–78
"Shake 'Em On Down," 189, 190
Sharecroppers, indebtedness of, 3–6, 31
Shaw, Robert, 43
Shirley, Maudie, 26, 27, 104, 107, 108, 111, 112, 138 passim
Short, J. D. "Jelly Jaw," 77
"Shotgun" houses, 7, 15
Simon, Joe, 73
Slavery, 25–26, 31, 122
Sledge, Miss., 190
"Slow drag" (dance), 45–46, 70, 92
Smith, Bessie Mae, 9, 27
"Smokey Mountain Blues," 15, 189
Snake, voodoo image in blues, 77, 109, 110, 120
Soul Children, 182
Soul music, 45–46, 47–48
South: black migration from, 6–7, 111; blues in, 25, 31, 35–36; racial taboos in, 11–12; sharecropping in, 31
Southern Railroad, 36, 127, 184
Spier, Henry, 8
Spirituals, 82, 192
Square dances, 96
Staple Singers, 80
Staples, "Pop," 80
Stories, as part of blues performances, 101
Suffering, theme of, in blues, hymns, slave songs, 31, 41, 48, 79–80
Sumner, Miss., 109, 128
Sunflower River, 32
"Sunny Road," 109, 192, 193
"Sweet Home," 95, 189
"Swing Low Sweet Chariot," 95, 190

Sykes, Roosevelt, 109, 127, 189, 191, 192, 193
Syrians, in Miss., 7

Taylor, Cal, 34
Tchula, Miss., 101
"Tennessee Waltz," 95, 189
Terrible Slug (blues singer), 104
Texas, 127
Texas Slim (John Lee Hooker), 77, 187, 188
"Think You Need a Shot (the Needle)," 187, 193
Thomas, Christine, 13, 14
Thomas, Earlie Mae "Ninnie," 45, 176, 185
Thomas, Floyd, 103, 104, 108, 111, 112, 113, 124 passim
Thomas, James "Son" (or "Cairo"), 3, 13–15, 21, 22, 23–34, 26, 27–28, 28–29, 38–39, 45–46, 49–50, 51–52, 58–59, 61–62, 64–65, 67–70, 79, 81, 85–86, 91, 92–93, 95, 96, 101–2, 160, 161, 174, 175, 176, 177, 188–89
Toasts, 108, 191
Tobe, Gussie, 15–16, 21–22, 41, 160–61
Trinidad, work songs in, 183
Tutwiler, Miss., 6, 8, 36, 96, 109, 128, 184

Verses (blues): and blues "talk," 103, 104–5, 107–13, 115 passim; composition of, xi, 61–65, 67–71; disc jockeys' use of, 74–75; flexibility of, 57–59, 67–71, 80; humor in, 26; records as source of, influence on, 51–54, 57–59, 70–71; relationship to work songs and religious music, 32–33, 58, 79–86; sense of place in, 28; similarity to proverbs, 73; themes

in, 12, 15, 25–58, 31, 35, 41–43, 48, 61–62, 64, 67–70, 77–78, 79–80, 81, 91, 108, 110; voodoo and sexual images in, 77–78
Vicksburg, Miss., 3, 28, 59, 109, 110, 120, 121, 192
Vinson, Arthur, 82, 83–84, 185, 188
Violence, at blues sessions, 101–3
Voodoo, 77–78

"Wabash Cannonball," 95, 190
Walthall, Miss., 96
Walton, Mercy Dee, 183, 191
Washington, D.C., 17
Watson, J. D. "Sonny Boy," 62–64, 159, 160, 168–69, 170–73
Webster County, Miss., 96
West Africa, 32, 37
"What Goes Up Must Come Down," 73–74
White, Booker Washington "Bukka," 8, 179, 189, 190
Whites, 7, 8, 9, 11, 12, 91, 92, 95–97, 110
"Why I Sing the Blues," 28, 74–75
Williams, Arthur Lee, xii, 12, 47–48, 49, 52, 57, 80
Williams, "Big Joe," 46, 182, 184, 189, 190, 193
Williams, Enoch "Sonny Boy," 39
Williamson, Rice "Sonny Boy," 52, 182, 189
Women, theme of, in blues, 35, 42, 61–62, 108
Work songs, 31–36, 183
Wright, O. V. (soul singer), 48

Yazoo City, Miss., 39, 184
Yazoo Delta Railroad (Yellow Dog), 36
"You Are My Sunshine," 95, 189